FORTUNE TELLER,

AND

DREAMER'S DICTIONARY.

AN INTERPRETATION TO ALL QUESTIONS UPON THE DIFFERENT EVENTS AND SIT-
UATIONS OF LIFE; BUT MORE ESPECIALLY RELATING TO LOVE, COURTSHIP,
AND MARRIAGE; CONTAINING A COMPLETE DICTIONARY OF
DREAMS ALPHABETICALLY ARRANGED, WITH A CLEAR

INTERPRETATION OF EACH DREAM,

AND THE

LUCKY NUMBERS THAT BELONG TO THEM.

ALSO, SHOWING HOW TO TELL FORTUNES BY THE WONDERFUL AND MYSTERIOUS

LADIES' LOVE ORACLE,

HOW TO FORETELL THE SEX AND NUMBER OF CHILDREN; HOW TO MAKE A LOVER
OR SWEETHEART COME TO YOU; TO TELL WHETHER YOUR LOVER OR SWEET-
HEART LOVE YOU; HOW TO TELL ANY PERSON'S AGE; TO KNOW WHO
YOUR FUTURE HUSBAND WILL BE, AND HOW SOON YOU WILL BE
MARRIED: TO ASCERTAIN WHETHER YOUR HUSBAND OR WIFE
IS TRUE TO YOU; TO TELL WHETHER YOU WILL ENJOY YOUR
LOVE; HOW TO TELL FUTURE EVENTS WITH CARDS, DICE,
TEA AND COFFEE-GROUNDS, EGGS, APPLE-PARINGS,
AND THE LINES OF THE HAND; HOW TO TELL A PERSON'S CHARACTER BY MEANS
OF CABALISTIC CALCULATIONS; HOW TO READ FORTUNES BY THE
MOLES ON A PERSON'S BODY, ALSO EXPLAINING

THE ART OF DISCOVERING TRUTH FROM FALSEHOOD.

TOGETHER WITH A LIST OF UNLUCKY DAYS, AND A LIST OF DAYS AND HOURS USU-
ALLY CONSIDERED FORTUNATE WITH RESPECT TO COURTSHIP, MARRIAGE,
AND LOVE AFFAIRS IN GENERAL, WITH A COLLECTION OF
CHARMS AND CEREMONIES, ETC., ETC.

BY MADAME LE MARCHAND,

The Celebrated Parisian Fortune Teller.

ILLUSTRATED WITH NUMEROUS ENGRAVINGS.

APPLEWOOD BOOKS

BEDFORD, MASSACHUSETTS

Madam Le Marchand's Fortune Teller and Dreamer's Dictionary was originally published in 1863.

Thank you for purchasing an Applewood Book. Applewood reprints America's lively classics—books from the past that are still of interest to modern readers. For a free copy of our current catalog, write to:
Applewood Books, P.O. Box 365, Bedford, MA 01730.

ISBN 1-55709-309-1

CONTENTS.

Entered according to Act of Congress, in the year 1863, by

DICK & FITZGERALD,

In the Clerk's Office of the District Court of the United States, for the Southern District of New York.

LE MARCHAND'S

FORTUNE TELLER

AND

DREAM BOOK.

THE LADIES' LOVE ORACLE; OR, HOW TO TELL FORTUNES WITH DICE.

METHOD OF CONSULTING THE ORACLE.

AFTER having chosen among the questions given in pages 4, 5, 6, the one to which you desire the oracle to reply, throw three dice at hazard upon the table, count the number they give, and consult the tables, pages 7, 8, 9, 10, following the line of the number of the question unto the column in the head of which you find the number that the dice have thrown. The number, then, in the line of the question, under the number the dice have given you, indicates the page where you will find the answer.

From the following example, you will see how easy this method is to follow. I suppose, among the things you desire most to know, the following question is not the least important:

Shall I be soon married?

You see that this is the first in the list of questions. Throw the three dice upon the table; they will give you, I suppose, seventeen; look in the table for the number of the question, which is 1; follow the line bearing at the top the number 17, which is the one the dice have given, and you will find in the same line as the number of the question, and beneath 17, the number 6, which is that of the page containing the answer; turn to page 6, look down the row of dice, until you find those representing the number 17, and you will find this reply:

"Yes, to the little dark-complexioned man."

Thus, you see, the operation is easy, quick, and simple. Whenever you wish to decide any question concerning your fate, you can consult the oracle, and know, without being obliged to confide your secrets to any person.

QUESTIONS TO WHICH THE ORACLE REPLIES.

1. Shall I be soon married?
2. Shall I receive what is promised me?
3. Is my love well-founded?
4. Who is my rival?
5. Where will my pranks lead me?
6. Shall I have children?
7. Will my husband love me?
8. Shall I go soon to the ball?
9. Is my secret well kept?
10. Shall I be again reconciled with him?
11. Will he not betray me?
12. What is a wise woman?
13. Will my husband be rich?
14. How can I keep them all?
15. Am I to marry?
16. By what shall I captivate him?
17. Am I to believe what is told me?
18. What will be my greatest fault?
19. Shall I accept his proposal?
20. Does my dress become me?
21. When shall I cease to weep?
22. Shall I write to him?
23. Must I pardon him?
24. Shall I succeed in my undertaking?
25. Shall I be fortunate at play?
26. When will he return?
27. Am I to go and meet him?

28. Does he love me sincerely?
29. Shall I go to the country?
30. Will my wishes be granted?
31. What is he doing?
32. What will my future be?
33. Is he discreet?
34. Shall I become a widow?
35. Which shall I take—the dark or fair?
36. Will he come?
37. Will my husband be young?
38. Oracle! am I pretty?
39. When shall I die?
40. Must I be cruel?
41. How can I make him love me?
42. When shall I begin to grow old?
43. How will this intrigue end?
44. Are all husbands alike?
45. Which is the happiest state?
46. Will my tricks be discovered?
47. Shall I marry the one I love?
48. Shall I quarrel with him?
49. Will he write to me?
50. Will my family approve my choice?
51. Shall I receive good news?
52. Shall I give him some hope?
53. What does society think of me?
54. Shall I change my conduct?
55. Shall I soon have an estate?
56. Whence comes my melancholy?
57. How shall I silence gossip?
58. What is love?
59. Shall I be fickle?
60. Shall I love a soldier?
61. Are not my advances imprudent?
62. What is life?
63. What shall I do to end my sorrows?
64. Shall I obtain rank?
65. Shall I improve my youth?

66. Shall I lose my law-suit?
67. What is a good husband?
68. Ought I to keep my promise?
69. Must I tell him my secret?
70. What is wisdom?
71. What is my principal fault?
72. Where is he?
73. Does gold confer happiness?
74. Am I witty?
75. Do all women resemble me?
76. Shall I live in the city or country?
77. Where shall I find happiness?
78. Will my happiness last?
79. Have I many enemies?
80. Shall I prefer love to money?

No. of Question	3	4	5	6	7	8	9	10	11	12	13	14	15	16	17	18
1	16	21	26	31	36	41	46	51	56	61	66	71	76	1	6	11
2	17	22	27	32	37	42	47	52	57	62	67	72	77	2	7	12
3	18	23	28	33	38	43	48	53	58	63	68	73	78	3	8	13
4	19	24	29	34	39	44	49	54	59	64	69	74	79	4	9	14
5	20	25	30	35	40	45	50	55	60	65	70	75	80	5	10	15
6	21	26	31	36	41	46	51	56	61	66	71	76	1	6	11	16
7	22	27	32	37	42	47	52	57	62	67	72	77	2	7	12	17
8	23	28	33	38	43	48	53	58	63	68	73	78	3	8	13	18
9	24	29	34	39	44	49	54	59	64	69	74	79	4	9	14	19
10	25	30	35	40	45	50	55	60	65	70	75	80	5	10	15	20
11	26	31	36	41	46	51	56	61	66	71	76	1	6	11	16	21
12	27	32	37	42	47	52	57	62	67	72	77	2	7	12	17	22
13	28	33	38	43	48	53	58	63	68	73	78	3	8	13	18	23
14	29	34	39	44	49	54	59	64	69	74	79	4	9	14	19	24
15	30	35	40	45	50	55	60	65	70	75	80	5	10	15	20	25
16	31	36	41	46	51	56	61	66	71	76	1	6	11	16	21	26
17	32	37	42	47	52	57	62	67	72	77	2	7	12	17	22	27
18	33	38	43	48	53	58	63	68	73	78	3	8	13	18	23	28
19	34	39	44	49	54	59	64	69	74	79	4	9	14	19	24	29
20	35	40	45	50	55	60	65	70	75	80	5	10	15	20	25	30

No. of Question	3	4	5	6	7	8	9	10	11	12	13	14	15	16	17	18
21	36	41	46	51	56	61	66	71	76	1	6	11	16	21	26	31
22	37	42	47	52	57	62	67	72	77	2	7	12	17	22	27	32
23	38	43	48	53	58	63	68	73	78	3	8	13	18	23	28	33
24	39	44	49	54	59	64	69	74	79	4	9	14	19	24	29	34
25	40	45	50	55	60	65	70	75	80	5	10	15	20	25	30	35
26	41	46	51	56	61	66	71	76	1	6	11	16	21	26	31	36
27	42	47	52	57	62	67	72	77	2	7	12	17	22	27	32	37
28	43	48	53	58	63	68	73	78	3	8	13	18	23	28	33	38
29	44	49	54	59	64	69	74	79	4	9	14	19	24	29	34	39
30	45	50	55	60	65	70	75	80	5	10	15	20	25	30	35	40
31	46	51	56	61	66	71	76	1	6	11	16	21	26	31	36	41
32	47	52	57	62	67	72	77	2	7	12	17	22	27	32	37	42
33	48	53	58	63	68	73	78	3	8	13	18	23	28	33	38	43
34	49	54	59	64	69	74	79	4	9	14	19	24	29	34	39	44
35	50	55	60	65	70	75	80	5	10	15	20	25	30	35	40	45
36	51	56	61	66	71	76	1	6	11	16	21	26	31	36	41	46
37	52	57	62	67	72	77	2	7	12	17	22	27	32	37	42	47
38	53	58	63	68	73	78	3	8	13	18	23	28	33	38	43	48
39	54	59	64	69	74	79	4	9	14	19	24	29	34	39	44	49
40	55	60	65	70	75	80	5	10	15	20	25	30	35	40	45	50

No. of Question	3	4	5	6	7	8	9	10	11	12	13	14	15	16	17	18
41	56	61	66	71	76	1	6	11	16	21	26	31	36	41	46	51
42	57	62	67	72	77	2	7	12	17	22	27	32	37	42	47	52
43	58	63	68	73	78	3	8	13	18	23	28	33	38	43	48	53
44	59	64	69	74	79	4	9	14	19	24	29	34	39	44	49	54
45	60	65	70	75	80	5	10	15	20	25	30	35	40	45	50	55
46	61	66	71	76	1	6	11	16	21	26	31	36	41	46	51	56
47	62	67	72	77	2	7	12	17	22	27	32	37	42	47	52	57
48	63	68	73	78	3	8	13	18	23	28	33	38	43	48	53	58
49	64	69	74	79	4	9	14	19	24	29	34	39	44	49	54	59
50	65	70	75	80	5	10	15	20	25	30	35	40	45	50	55	60
51	66	71	76	1	6	11	16	21	26	31	36	41	46	51	56	61
52	67	72	77	2	7	12	17	22	27	32	37	42	47	52	57	62
53	68	73	78	3	8	13	18	23	28	33	38	43	48	53	58	63
54	69	74	79	4	9	14	19	24	29	34	39	44	49	54	59	64
55	70	75	80	5	10	15	20	25	30	35	40	45	50	55	60	65
56	71	76	1	6	11	16	21	26	31	36	41	46	51	56	61	66
57	72	77	2	7	12	17	22	27	32	37	42	47	52	57	62	67
58	73	78	3	8	13	18	23	28	33	38	43	48	53	58	63	68
59	74	79	4	9	14	19	24	29	34	39	44	49	54	59	64	69
60	75	80	5	10	15	20	25	30	35	40	45	50	55	60	65	70

No. of Question	3	4	5	6	7	8	9	10	11	12	13	14	15	16	17	18
61	76	1	6	11	16	21	26	31	36	41	46	51	56	61	66	71
62	77	2	7	12	17	22	27	32	37	42	47	52	57	62	67	72
63	78	3	8	13	18	23	28	33	38	43	48	53	58	63	68	73
64	79	4	9	14	19	24	29	34	39	44	49	54	59	64	69	74
65	80	5	10	15	20	25	30	35	40	45	50	55	60	65	70	75
66	1	6	11	16	21	26	31	36	41	46	51	56	61	66	71	76
67	2	7	12	17	22	27	32	37	42	47	52	57	62	67	72	77
68	3	8	13	18	23	28	33	38	43	48	53	58	63	68	73	78
69	4	9	14	19	24	29	34	39	44	49	54	59	64	69	74	79
70	5	10	15	20	25	30	35	40	45	50	55	60	65	70	75	80
71	6	11	16	21	26	31	36	41	46	51	56	61	66	71	76	1
72	7	12	17	22	27	32	37	42	47	52	57	62	67	72	77	2
73	8	13	18	23	28	33	38	43	48	53	58	63	68	73	78	3
74	9	14	19	24	29	34	39	44	49	54	59	64	69	74	79	4
75	10	15	20	25	30	35	40	45	50	55	60	65	70	75	80	5
76	11	16	21	26	31	36	41	46	51	56	61	66	71	76	1	6
77	12	17	22	27	32	37	42	47	52	57	62	67	72	77	2	7
78	13	18	23	28	33	38	43	48	53	58	63	68	73	78	3	8
79	14	19	24	29	34	39	44	49	54	59	64	69	74	79	4	9
80	15	20	25	30	35	40	45	50	55	60	65	70	75	80	5	10

ANSWERS TO THE ORACLE.

Your cause is just, you will gain it.

Be careful, you are watched.

By his inconstancy.

She will cause you much sorrow.

Your conduct will open their eyes.

By the means you employ for others.

Yes, in an hour.

Nothing good.

The day of his arrival.

When you shall have forgotten it.

By a little more condescension.

Oh, my dear, unworthily.

Yes, twins.

No your faults are too well known.

Live where the one you love does.

Idleness.

Your own.

A taper threatened to extinguish it.

In outcrying the slanderers.

It will be too glorious.

Yes, if you persist.

Not before fifty years.

Yes, very young.

It will be unfruitful.

Go to your ruin, if you will.

Imprudent.

He always speaks the truth.

What you will one day become.

It is needful that he be very good.

Yes, in spite of delays.

Ask thy gallant.

Where his misdeeds have led him.

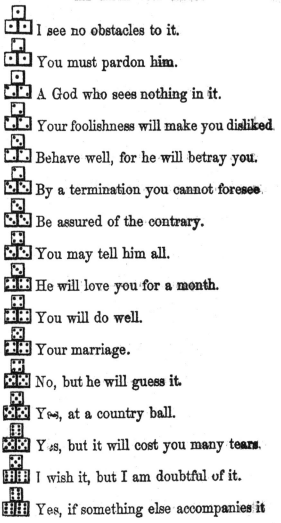

I see no obstacles to it.

You must pardon him.

A God who sees nothing in it.

Your foolishness will make you disliked.

Behave well, for he will betray you.

By a termination you cannot foresee.

Be assured of the contrary.

You may tell him all.

He will love you for a month.

You will do well.

Your marriage.

No, but he will guess it.

Yes, at a country ball.

Yes, but it will cost you many tears.

I wish it, but I am doubtful of it.

Yes, if something else accompanies it

Wait a few months **longer.**

Yes, to-night.

No, it would be **wrong.**

Yes, to avoid scandal.

Yes, what he does not think **of.**

Your mother will tell it to **him.**

Do not be uneasy.

No.

Go, happiness awaits you there

Yes, if you are skillful.

You would be **wrong.**

By appearing frank and **open.**

Yes, my beauty.

An afflicted woman, nineteen **years old**

Yes, but do not fear them.

Yes, the wittiest of **women**

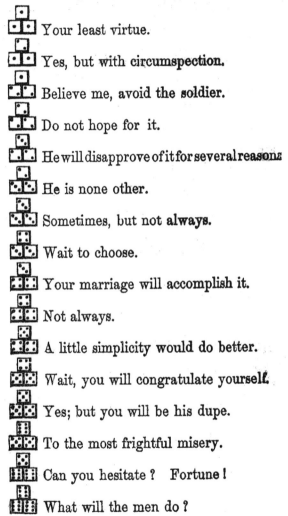

Your least virtue.

Yes, but with circumspection.

Believe me, avoid the soldier.

Do not hope for it.

He will disapprove of it for several reasons

He is none other.

Sometimes, but not always.

Wait to choose.

Your marriage will accomplish it.

Not always.

A little simplicity would do better.

Wait, you will congratulate yourself.

Yes; but you will be his dupe.

To the most frightful misery.

Can you hesitate ?   Fortune !

What will the men do ?

Avarice.

Your enemy is powerful

Yes, now and then.

From your jealousy.

No, my fine lady.

Be upon your guard.

Do you not know it?

He has other visits to make.

He is at the feet of your rival.

One hour before your marriage

When you shall have what you wish

By a more careful toilet.

He loves you too much for that.

Yes, by bewitching him.

Yes, to the little dark-complexioned man

In the country you will die of weariness

Far from here.

He who is not jealous.

A trifle upon which you stand.

Scorn them.

It would be being too coquettish.

You are mistress of it.

Your mirror will tell you so.

A little upon the decay.

It will be very brilliant.

That would be very dangerous.

No, it would be too glorious.

If you do not fear him, you are lost.

The most resigned.

Yes, until death.

Without doubt.

In work.

Not always.

Yes, if you wish it.

You must be resigned.

One guided by folly.

You are very amiable.

Do you wish for him ?

The wine is drawn, you must drink it.

You have been so, but are no longer

Would he wish it ?

He is not fool enough for that

He merits it.

Refusing the one who presents himself

Yes, but silly.

Yes, to make you laugh at your enemies

Calm your fears.

Unfortunately no

Be careful about believing him.

Do not this foolishness.

No, my love.

Your heart is closed to him.

Yes, little by little.

Yes, but very rarely.

They are more or less amiable.

Expect death, but do not fear it.

Marry, and I will tell it you

No, remain in the city.

You will be disappointed.

Yes, if that will serve you.

By making strong professions.

Not extremely well.

The prima donna of a foreign theatre

As many friends.

Resembling you slightly.

What you have not and will never have

Yes, because they will pass quickly

Wouldst thou prefer a uniform ?

Yes, from an uncle in California.

Hope.

Your own.

Why delay your happiness ?

The dark-complexioned deceives you

Yes. if you marry.

Play will ruin you.

No, you have too bad a figure.

Yes, to be happy.

Do not this folly.

Crime.

Between the two you cannot choose.

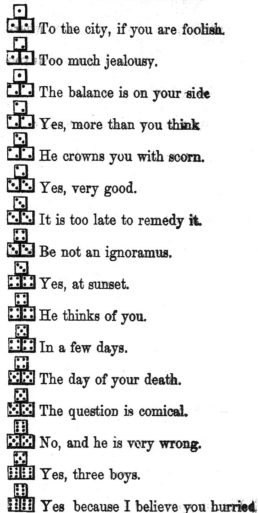

To the city, if you are foolish.

Too much jealousy.

The balance is on your side

Yes, more than you think

He crowns you with scorn.

Yes, very good.

It is too late to remedy it.

Be not an ignoramus.

Yes, at sunset.

He thinks of you.

In a few days.

The day of your death.

The question is comical.

No, and he is very wrong.

Yes, three boys.

Yes because I believe you hurried

Nowhere, you are wearied everywhere.

His body is far, but his heart is near you

He who is destined for you.

Something everybody fears to lose.

Your reputation is above all.

Why deceive him ?

Do not doubt it.

Wrinkles in your face will announce it.

He will have passed forty.

The horizon is very dark.

Be distrustful, it is a trap.

Go rather to speak to him

You can, without danger.

Every one is ignorant of it.

No he will prefer wine.

Yes, on your birthday.

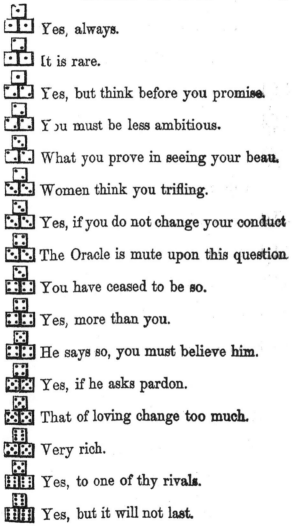

Yes, always.

It is rare.

Yes, but think before you promise.

You must be less ambitious.

What you prove in seeing your beau.

Women think you trifling.

Yes, if you do not change your conduct.

The Oracle is mute upon this question.

You have ceased to be so.

Yes, more than you.

He says so, you must believe him.

Yes, if he asks pardon.

That of loving change too much.

Very rich.

Yes, to one of thy rivals.

Yes, but it will not last.

You need not fear those you have.

Wit turns your head.

Yes, but hide nothing from him.

Your most precious jewel will be stolen

Yes, from time to time.

Without doubt.

Yes, to tell you what you know

Yes, all as simple.

Your life will be long and happy

How curious you are!

You will incur great danger.

Do not be uneasy.

Give yourself this satisfaction.

Do not try it, you will fail.

Enough for its importance.

The rival of Madame Blanc.

Prefer fortune, it is the most lasting.

All have not your wit.

The most of the Creator's gifts.

Yes, it is time for it.

A cavalry officer will charm you.

Not before twenty.

Interest will guide her.

Prudence forbids me to tell you.

Yes, from time to time.

The bionde does not love you.

It is impossible.

Yes, if you cheat.

Yes, ugliness adorned appears handsome

Prefer celibacy to marriage.

Yes, very near.

Perhaps to the scaffold ! ! ! !

That will depend on yourself.

Everywhere you will shine.

Coquetry.

No, if you speak the truth.

Yes, act with more reflection.

To see your rival triumph.

Let not that disturb you.

They will be so by a friend.

By promising all.

Yes, in a minute.

He will commit suicide.

Later than you think.

Very near.

How simple you are !

Yes, but pardon him.

Yes, four daughters.

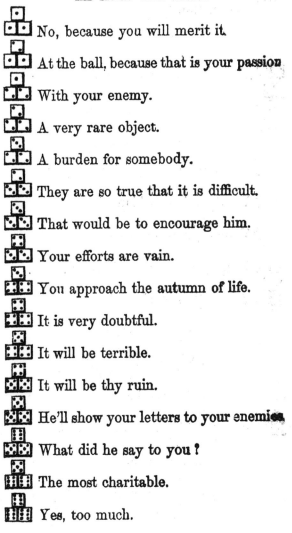

No, because you will merit it.

At the ball, because that is your passion.

With your enemy.

A very rare object.

A burden for somebody.

They are so true that it is difficult.

That would be to encourage him.

Your efforts are vain.

You approach the autumn of life.

It is very doubtful.

It will be terrible.

It will be thy ruin.

He'll show your letters to your enemies.

What did he say to you?

The most charitable.

Yes, too much.

Yes, without doubt.

As long as thy youth.

That will depend on circumstances.

No, if you wish to remain virtuous

Renounce your projects.

What you would wish to inspire.

Your conduct is blamed.

Your reputation exacts it.

Very badly.

Yes, with a mask.

Like the reeds of Phrygia.

I do not believe it.

That would save his life.

That would reveal your secret.

Yes, rich and amiable.

You will he invited. but do not go

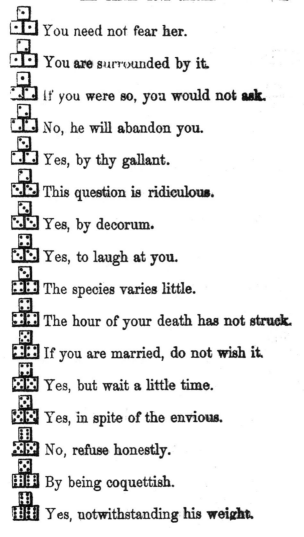

You need not fear her.

You are surrounded by it.

If you were so, you would not ask.

No, he will abandon you.

Yes, by thy gallant.

This question is ridiculous.

Yes, by decorum.

Yes, to laugh at you.

The species varies little.

The hour of your death has not struck.

If you are married, do not wish it.

Yes, but wait a little time.

Yes, in spite of the envious.

No, refuse honestly.

By being coquettish.

Yes, notwithstanding his weight.

For repentance.

Love is preferable, if it is sincere.

What will become of the husbands.

What you know not how to gain.

Can you ask the question?

An artillery-man will take your heart

Yes, but others will profit by it.

Your choice is very bad.

You will know it very soon.

Later.

The dark complexion will be rich.

Yes, I swear it to you.

If you have reason, do not play.

She will not make you handsome.

No, not yet.

Yes, if you take the first step.

Much.

In a short time, you will be madame.

You will be more free in the country.

Pride.

Not if you have a good lawyer.

Be reassured, they are not so.

The most trifling things.

They cannot fail of being so.

Yes, you will have this trouble.

In conforming yourself to his wishes

Perhaps this evening.

His will.

St. John's day

When you are less perverse

By your virtues.

Yes, and he does well.

Yes, if your conduct is irreproachable.

Yes, if you are wise.

To innocent sports.

To the ball with a young black-eyed lady

Marry, and you will know it.

A comedy in several acts.

Your marriage will silence them.

Yes, but take care.

Happily, no.

If I tell you, you will hate me.

He'll be between twenty and sixty years

It will be sown with roses and thorns.

You will not find him there.

Do not write, or you are lost.

Yes, but not all.

It is you, my lady.

Prepare yourself.

Be assured of the contrary.

Yes, a month or more.

Yes, that of the ambitious.

No, this would be your loss.

Be less jealous, and you will be happy.

Something that does not really exist.

You are judged with indulgence.

Yes, to silence slanderers.

Very well.

Yes, to pilfer.

Yes, very discreet.

It is certain he knows you slightly.

Let him be pardoned.

Forget him for your happiness

Yes, in hopes.

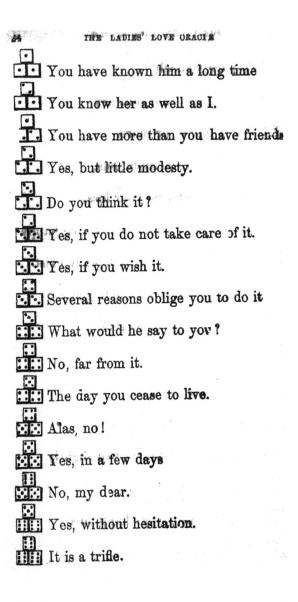

You have known him a long time

You know her as well as I.

You have more than you have friends

Yes, but little modesty.

Do you think it?

Yes, if you do not take care of it.

Yes, if you wish it.

Several reasons oblige you to do it

What would he say to you?

No, far from it.

The day you cease to live.

Alas, no!

Yes, in a few days

No, my dear.

Yes, without hesitation.

It is a trifle.

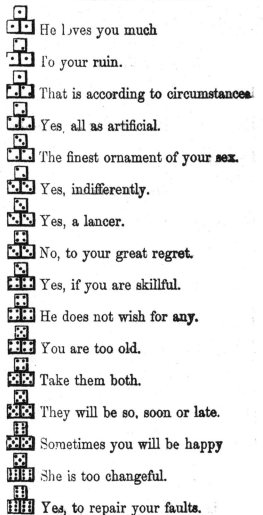

He loves you much

To your ruin.

That is according to circumstances

Yes, all as artificial.

The finest ornament of your sex.

Yes, indifferently.

Yes, a lancer.

No, to your great regret.

Yes, if you are skillful.

He does not wish for any.

You are too old.

Take them both.

They will be so, soon or late.

Sometimes you will be happy

She is too changeful.

Yes, to repair your faults.

Could he do otherwise ?

More than you wish of it.

Thirty years from now.

In the city, if you like an exciting life

Vanity.

No, and his loss will ruin you.

Yes, but no attention is paid to it.

By a desire you cannot satisfy.

Much better than the last.

Yes, by your marriage.

By removing your rivals.

Yes, to break with you.

He fights a duel for you.

To-morrow morning.

Soon, if you change your conduct.

The sight of you will charm him.

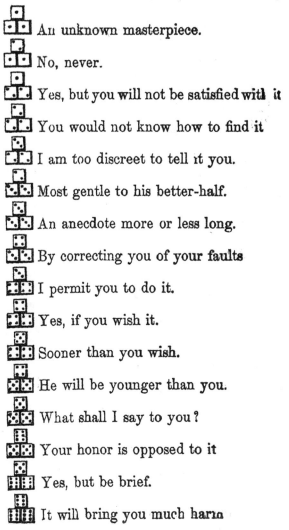

An unknown masterpiece.

No, never.

Yes, but you will not be satisfied with it

You would not know how to find it

I am too discreet to tell it you.

Most gentle to his better-half.

An anecdote more or less long.

By correcting you of your faults

I permit you to do it.

Yes, if you wish it.

Sooner than you wish.

He will be younger than you.

What shall I say to you?

Your honor is opposed to it

Yes, but be brief.

It will bring you much harm

Have you need to be happy?

Yes, to make tapestry.

It might be better placed.

Not very long.

Ask it of the Fates.

You would incur too many obligations

You must yield to cirumstances.

A thing that time removes.

They find you very ridiculous.

Appear to wish to break with him.

By a quarrel.

Yes, when you are overburdened

A secret is a burden to him.

Yes, with all his manly heart.

Be not insensible to his tears.

Being too prudish with him.

Coquette! will not one suffice?

Everybody knows it.

You would be angry if I told you.

Yes, and much exasperated.

Frankly, I do not believe it.

Which?

Be assured you will not be so.

Yes, but only in love.

It is time

Yes, to make you a thousand promises

Yes, all the same.

Never, you are immortal.

Yes, after being married seventy years.

Yes, in a numerous company.

When near to success you will fail.

Yes, if you believe him sincere.

Consult your heart.

Could he live without you?

To a premature old age.

Neither will make you happy.

All have not your virtues.

A very rare virtue.

Do it to suit yourself.

Soldiers change garrisons often.

Imprudent one what do you wish?

She would disapprove of it.

Marriage.

Why make him a martyr?

Neither.

No, they are too ambitious.

You will lose your patrimony.

It will give you a very plain appearance

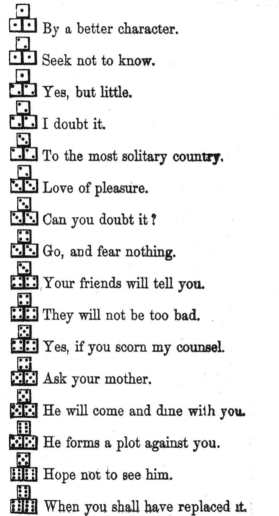

By a better character.

Seek not to know.

Yes, but little.

I doubt it.

To the most solitary country.

Love of pleasure.

Can you doubt it ?

Go, and fear nothing.

Your friends will tell you.

They will not be too bad.

Yes, if you scorn my counsel.

Ask your mother.

He will come and dine with you.

He forms a plot against you.

Hope not to see him.

When you shall have replaced it.

Not if you are wise.

The most discreet.

Yes, because you deserve it.

Perhaps.

You will not ask this after this evening.

He is engaged in a revel.

They are no longer found in this country.

A meadow that death mows.

Be resigned, it is impossible.

Watch over yourself.

Many obstacles will hinder you.

She will soon commence.

Young enough to think you old.

Curiosity, I will tell you nothing.

Go there with your friend.

Yes, but do not sign it.

What you will do this evening.

You are busy with useless things.

Yes, but wear a mask.

Go always.

It will last a short time.

The fool says yes, the wise man no.

The wine is drawn, you must drink it.

Nothing, they are chimeras.

A history sometimes tragic.

Your pride is laughed at.

You will find as good a one.

There will be no sad consequences.

You would be so, if you were less ugly

No, and he will do it honor.

Yes, for he thinks you wise.

No, his fault is unpardonable.

Why not ?

Impossible, you are too awkward.

It is too weighty to keep.

What a question!　You have none

No, but some enemies.

You should be a little more so.

Yes, if you have a conscience.

It is very possible.

Constancy belongs to your years

Believe me, always go.

Yes, to reproach you

Yes, all as stupid.

Past twenty-four years.

Yes, but at an advanced age.

My child, I do not believe it

Yes, if you follow the right way

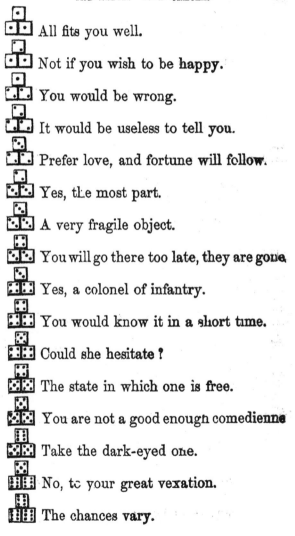

All fits you well.

Not if you wish to be **happy.**

You would be wrong.

It would be useless to tell **you.**

Prefer love, and fortune will **follow.**

Yes, the most part.

A very fragile object.

You will go there too late, **they are gone.**

Yes, a colonel of infantry.

You would know it in **a short time.**

Could she hesitate ?

The state in which one is **free.**

You are not a good enough **comedienne**

Take the dark-eyed one.

No, to your great **vexation.**

The chances **vary.**

Never.

By more modesty.

Faint-hearted! are you suspicious?

I will tell you to-morrow, if you are wise.

No, because you are too inconstant.

In the city for thirty years.

That of being too fickle.

A false witness will make you lose all

I will tell you when they are so.

It would be too long to tell you.

You will receive some excellent ones.

You ought to expect it there.

In lending himself to your humors.

Yes, since he has promised you.

He smokes his segar and forgets you

To-morrow or never

Keep yourself free from it.

No, he deceives you.

The philosopher's stone for husbands

Yes, a little.

Count no more upon it.

In the society where you are an ornament

He scours the country for news.

The least willful.

A voyage fruitful in accidents.

With uprightness and perseverance.

It is useless.

Impossible, he loves another of them.

In a little.

Yes, young, rich, and amiable.

Your future ? it will be sad.

Yes, if you are sure of yourself

3

Not yet, it is too soon.

That of scorning my counsel.

Yes, but you will ruin him.

Yes, to meet your rivals there.

No, because he is tardy.

No, by your fault.

Yes, if you make good use of it.

No, my dear.

You must renounce the world.

A child whom you must mistrust.

A dangerous good.

Yes, break with him.

Very well, if you manage skillfully.

Handsome body, but deformed mind

He is, and will be so always.

Yes, but it will not be eternal.

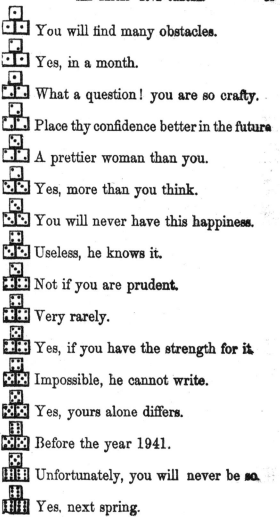

You will find many obstacles.

Yes, in a month.

What a question! you are so crafty.

Place thy confidence better in the future

A prettier woman than you.

Yes, more than you think.

You will never have this happiness.

Useless, he knows it.

Not if you are prudent.

Very rarely.

Yes, if you have the strength for it.

Impossible, he cannot write.

Yes, yours alone differs.

Before the year 1941.

Unfortunately, you will never be so.

Yes, next spring.

Play, but with moderation.

That depends on circumstances.

Be sure not to do it, you are too fickle

Replace him, he will never return.

To a return of wisdom.

Prefer fortune, ambition bids it.

This would be an affliction.

A difficult path to follow.

Yes, these pleasures suit your age.

With a juggler you will visit many lands

You will inherit from a friend

No, it will be disapproved.

The state of innocence.

Yes, during a few days.

Take the fair one.

Yes, to dry your tears.

Too soon.

When you are wiser.

By a little less prudering.

Continue to ignore him.

All, believe it.

Do not count upon it.

I advise you to live in a city.

I know none of them.

A mysterious person will help you gain it

Not at all.

Can you not guess?

Unfortunately, no.

Not if you are circumspect.

By making him many promises

No, he has ceased to love you.

Much evil.

Yes, if you please.

It would be inconvenient.

Believe his words, they are sincere

An unfound treasure.

Not much.

You are not then to get it.

In your boudoir.

At the feet of his new conquest

The most foolish.

A river of honey and vinegar

By flying from the cause.

Yes, but do not yield.

No, because I do not wish it.

Fear nothing, you are yet young.

He will be old, poor, and deformed.

Most happy.

Seek not to know it.

That will depend on his conduct.

You are too wise to commit one.

Were he rich he would not marry you

Yes, but do not dance there.

Yes, you are paid back.

You have yet many trials in store.

To believe it would be folly.

Follow my counsel.

You must leave the city.

A skillful archer.

They think you foolish.

With which ?

By a duel, in which your friend will fall

Yes, but you are too proud of it

Discretion is her only virtue.

Yes, next month.

Do not count upon it.

That would be foolish.

By yielding all.

He could not be better trusted.

A frank, sincere man of forty years

Mistrust them, they are numerous.

Thy wit equals thy beauty.

Yes, if you have the courage for it.

No, but you will steal—hearts.

You can until thirty years.

Yes, if you wish to find a husband.

Why should he write to you ?

Women would be too much to be pitied.

Before one hundred years.

Dear friend, I despair of it.

Yes, all except one.

You will make your fortune there.

No, you wear it so awkwardly.

Marriage is worse than the plague.

Yes, if you can bring him back to you

Alas! could you not foresee it?

Love.

Few are as inconstant.

A vessel that often makes shipwreck

Yes, but fear the consequences.

Yes, a hussar.

From whence should he come to you?

Rejoice, she will approve of it.

For you, the cloister.

Yes, if you have strength for it

The dark-eyed one will be most faithful

3*

He will forget you.

To-morrow he will be at your feet

When you shall be married

By a little foresight.

You must be resigned.

Yes, but only two.

Be not in so much of a hurry.

You will find happiness in the country

Slander.

Yes, but it would be unjust.

They can be no more so.

By a foolish fear.

Yes, but they will be false.

Let not this fear worry you

By feigning to love another.

Don't wait for it, you'll only lose time

It will be as the past.

What would you do **there ?**

Why not?

You cannot too much mistrust his **words**

She who does not **resemble you.**

Surely.

Be persuaded of it.

The question is **simple.**

With a titled friend.

The most credulous.

A bitter and narcotic **plant.**

By a less equivocal **manner.**

Yes, but very little.

Yes, in spite of envy.

You should not think of it at your **age**

Yes, but very ugly.

Very little.

In his heart he detests you.

He is too ungrateful.

To yield too easily.

Yes, richer than you.

Could he have one without you?

He could not be better.

Yes, if you moderate your enjoyments

Gold is a chimera.

You cannot dispense with it.

To be married.

The most severe disease.

Your pretensions are laughed at.

Yes. if you have the courage for it.

By a marriage and a baptism.

Not as much as you presume.

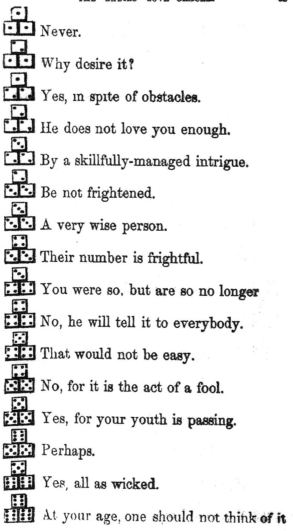

Never.

Why desire it?

Yes, in spite of obstacles.

He does not love you enough.

By a skillfully-managed intrigue.

Be not frightened.

A very wise person.

Their number is frightful.

You were so, but are so no longer

No, he will tell it to everybody.

That would not be easy.

No, for it is the act of a fool.

Yes, for your youth is passing.

Perhaps.

Yes, all as wicked.

At your age, one should not think of it

Take the most fashionable.

Their accomplishment will cost you dear

This passion will make you unhappy.

Wonderfully well

Yes, but the latest possible.

He does not think of you.

In a few years you will know.

I have told you, gold gives not happiness

None are so prudish.

The enemy of folly.

Yes, because they will not last long.

Your husband will belong to the 7th Reg

You will do both.

Yes, I promise it to you.

If you were loving you would know it.

You could only lose it there.

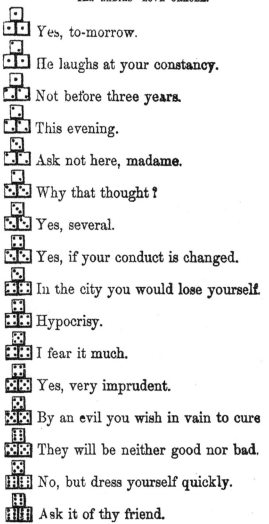

Yes, to-morrow.

He laughs at your constancy.

Not before three years.

This evening.

Ask not here, madame.

Why that thought?

Yes, several.

Yes, if your conduct is changed.

In the city you would lose yourself.

Hypocrisy.

I fear it much.

Yes, very imprudent.

By an evil you wish in vain to cure

They will be neither good nor bad.

No, but dress yourself quickly.

Ask it of thy friend.

Yes, too young for you.

He will be very fortunate.

Your heart ought to tell **you.**

It is useless.

I do not advise you to it.

An imaginary object.

Not at all.

Alas, no !

In the country.

In the garret of a dressmaker

A man a little foolish.

A too-short history.

By using skillful tactics.

Yes, if you wish to make him **happy.**

I give you my consent.

You will be fresh at sixty **years.**

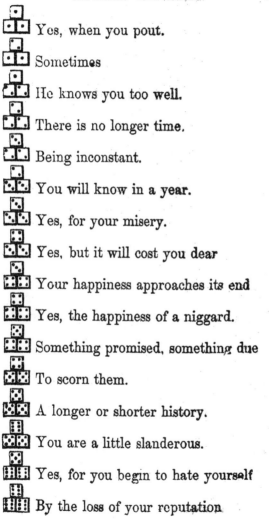

Yes, when you pout.

Sometimes

He knows you too well.

There is no longer time.

Being inconstant.

You will know in a year.

Yes, for your misery.

Yes, but it will cost you dear

Your happiness approaches its end

Yes, the happiness of a niggard.

Something promised, something due

To scorn them.

A longer or shorter history.

You are a little slanderous.

Yes, for you begin to hate yourself

By the loss of your reputation

When your last hour **shall come.**

To what good?

You please yourself **by it.**

A trifle will stop **you.**

Yes, but later.

You know your part, it is idle to teach you

Henceforth trust none with your secrets.

A lady with small feet.

Yes, but you will conquer all.

Enough for your position in the world

It is the way to quarrel with him.

Yes, to your great satisfaction ?

You are too unskillful.

Yes, bid adieu to lovers.

Yes, but do not read his letter

That would be desirable.

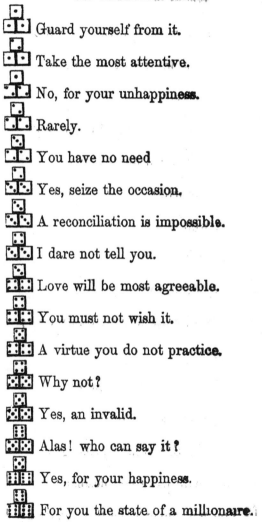

Guard yourself from it.

Take the most attentive.

No, for your unhappiness.

Rarely.

You have no need

Yes, seize the occasion.

A reconciliation is impossible.

I dare not tell you.

Love will be most agreeable.

You must not wish it.

A virtue you do not practice.

Why not?

Yes, an invalid.

Alas! who can say it?

Yes, for your happiness.

For you the state of a millionaire.

By making some advances to him

Yes, if he knows where to go.

He expects you.

A letter from him will tell you all.

Alas! who can foresee it?

By your wit.

You well deserve it.

Why not?

Many things are opposed to it.

You will be unfortunate in the city

Pride.

It is certain you will gain it.

Yes, a great deal too much.

By a youth too long prolonged.

They will make you desolate.

You will never have this vexation

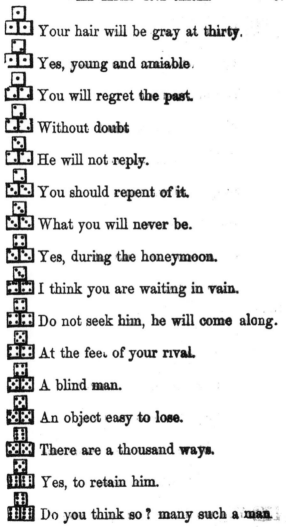

Your hair will be gray at **thirty**.

Yes, young and **amiable**.

You will regret **the past**.

Without **doubt**

He will not **reply**.

You should **repent of it**.

What you will **never be**.

Yes, during the honeymoon.

I think you are waiting in **vain**.

Do not seek him, he **will come** along.

At the feet of your **rival**.

A blind **man**.

An object easy **to lose**.

There are a thousand **ways**.

Yes, to retain him.

Do you think **so**? many such a **man**.

Did you not foresee it?

Those who say so are flatterers.

Tell him nothing,

Why not believe him?

Reflect before you act.

To quarrel with him.

No, it is no harm.

Not as soon as you wish

Indifferently.

Yes, if you are virtuous.

Alone, no.

What have you promised?

Tell me what causes them.

An idol that every one worships.

They call you charming.

You would be in despair about it.

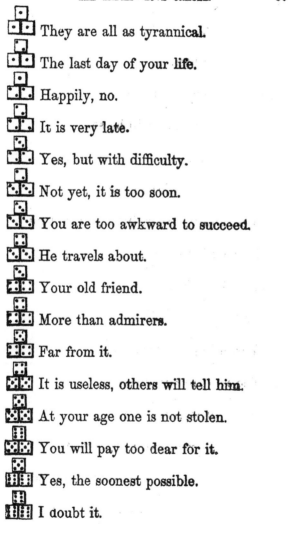

They are all as tyrannical.

The last day of your life.

Happily, no.

It is very late.

Yes, but with difficulty.

Not yet, it is too soon.

You are too awkward to succeed.

He travels about.

Your old friend.

More than admirers.

Far from it.

It is useless, others will tell him.

At your age one is not stolen.

You will pay too dear for it.

Yes, the soonest possible.

I doubt it.

Celibacy.

Not with him.

Make them draw lots.

Be patient, they will be so.

Very often.

How coquettish you are.

Yes, and together, because it is time

I forbid it to you.

To a terrible trial.

Prefer love, until you are thirty.

Yes, all as great coquettes.

The road to happiness.

Yes, but stop in time.

May God preserve you from it.

Ambitious one, have you not enough?

Yes, because it is excellent.

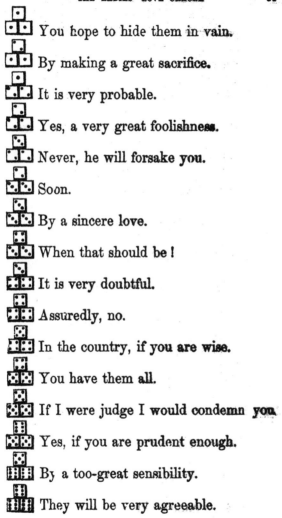

You hope to hide them in vain.

By making a great sacrifice.

It is very probable.

Yes, a very great foolishness.

Never, he will forsake you.

Soon.

By a sincere love.

When that should be !

It is very doubtful.

Assuredly, no.

In the country, if you are wise.

You have them all.

If I were judge I would condemn you.

Yes, if you are prudent enough.

By a too-great sensibility.

They will be very agreeable.

Yes, but it will be with difficulty.

At a very advanced age.

You will know in two months.

You will meet with many misfortunes

Could you do without it?

Not to-day.

Yes, if he perseveres.

The most constant.

Be easy, he will adore you.

I will tell it you to-morrow.

At the theater.

I dare not tell you.

Read "The Physiology of Marriage.

The servant of death.

By perseverance and skill.

Yes, to amuse him

Yes, for eight days.

By a great scandal.

Take a mirror.

Not too much.

Yes, for some time.

Impossible.

Coquetry.

Enough to satisfy your frivolous tastes

It is impossible.

Indifferently.

Yes, from midday to midnight.

Rarely.

Yes, but later.

Oh, many things.

It is slippery ground.

Your ignorance is laugned at.

Yes, from time to time.

No, yours is not as good as that of others

In a very long time.

You would be to be pitied.

Yes, if you love solitude.

Yes, in twenty years.

You would repent of it.

Experience alone will teach you

The self-confident is a great boaster.

Seek not to know it.

Yes, much

Enough to be amiable.

Yes, if you can without blushing.

Distrust yourself

You lack the means.

Yes, to make the past forgotten.

She would be wrong.

Widowhood.

The least possible.

The blonde is too young.

Hope.

Sometimes.

Not enough for ornament.

Be not so foolish.

He is anxious to repair the wrong

After the lightning comes thunder

Prefer love to fortune.

May we be kept from it.

What one loses when one loves.

No one weighs this question at your age

No, neither trumpet nor drum.

Yes, when you have more teeth.

Assuredly they will be good.

How could they not be so ?

Be patient, you will arrive at it in time

Do not wait for it.

Unfaithfulness.

Sunday, after church.

You have much trouble.

Consult his tastes.

Yes, very often.

You ought not to hope.

Not before the sixtieth.

The summer in the country

Indifference.

The answer is on page 41, No. 1.

Heigho ! I do not say no.

By your sadness.

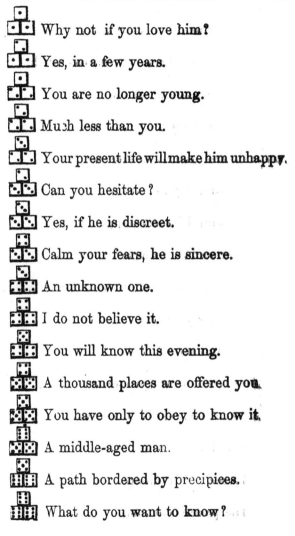

Why not if you love him?

Yes, in a few years.

You are no longer young.

Much less than you.

Your present life will make him unhappy.

Can you hesitate?

Yes, if he is discreet.

Calm your fears, he is sincere.

An unknown one.

I do not believe it.

You will know this evening.

A thousand places are offered you.

You have only to obey to know it.

A middle-aged man.

A path bordered by precipices.

What do you want to know?

They think you very witty.

Impossible, he loves you too much.

By a great misfortune.

Like an angel.

He has told me his secret.

He adores you.

He would be too happy.

That will be to deceive him.

Yes, but your extravagance will ruin h m

Not this year.

Not too much.

Yes, if you are prudent.

Sometimes, but not always.

Yes, but in secret.

To see him no more.

The pastime of fools.

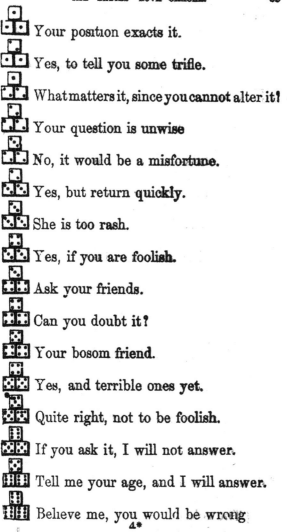

Your position exacts it.

Yes, to tell you some trifle.

What matters it, since you cannot alter it!

Your question is unwise

No, it would be a misfortune.

Yes, but return quickly.

She is too rash.

Yes, if you are foolish.

Ask your friends.

Can you doubt it?

Your bosom friend.

Yes, and terrible ones yet.

Quite right, not to be foolish.

If you ask it, I will not answer.

Tell me your age, and I will answer.

Believe me, you would be wrong

4*

Yes, but it will cost you many tears.

No, for she wishes your happiness.

Youth.

You will be sorry for it.

The dark-eyed one is too old.

Yes, in a few days.

You play too large a stake.

Much less than you think.

A fool would say yes, I say no.

That will be difficult.

All except goodness.

Fortune is nothing without love.

There are few as ridiculous.

What one rarely loves at your age.

Yes, profit by time.

The soldier is out of fashion.

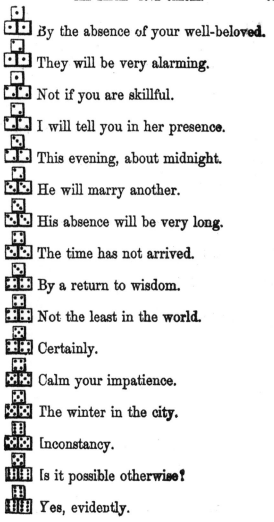

By the absence of your well-beloved.

They will be very alarming.

Not if you are skillful.

I will tell you in her presence.

This evening, about midnight.

He will marry another.

His absence will be very long.

The time has not arrived.

By a return to wisdom.

Not the least in the world.

Certainly.

Calm your impatience.

The winter in the city.

Inconstancy.

Is it possible otherwise?

Yes, evidently.

You will have much to do.

Certainly ; what do you risk ?

Your parents will oppose it.

It is no matter, you always complain

You will not reach eighty.

He'll be handsome, like your present one

Yes, but change the place for it.

He will not read your letter.

No, he flatters you too much

The least jealous.

Yes, but not long.

Not yet, but soon.

In exciting pleasures.

Upon the road to fame.

A man not clear-sighted.

Our treasure.

The tyrant of all hearts.

A very good one

Yes, by your fault.

By a scandalous quarrel

They tell you enough.

He would not know how to be so.

Not at once.

You would be his dupe.

She has committed herself, it is too late

Do not doubt it.

Your marriage day.

The future will teach you it.

Yes, if you behave wisely.

That depends on circumstances.

Wait, the pear is not ripe.

To be reconciled to him.

You will do well to abstain from it.

Your conscience ought to guide you.

Yes, a letter as monotonous as himself

Ask your friends.

Do not torment yourself.

You ought not to wish it.

Yes, very soon.

Appearances are against it.

Do what you will, he will deceive you.

Act with cunning and you will succeed

Far from it.

An actress.

Enough to ruin you.

Your face shows it a little.

Your honor requires it.

Already you are so.

Yes, a light and deceitful cavalier

Fortunately not so soon.

Do not hope it.

That depends on taste.

For what use?

The blonde is the most amiable

Yes, in a few years.

What game?

Is it possible otherwise?

That would be a wise act.

Do not hope it.

To a dreadful end.

That depends on your age

Can you presume so?

You will never know it.

You consult me too late.

Yes, they excite many slanders.

By a loving spite.

Yes, excellent.

They are already so.

Your heart ought to guide you

Yes, but be prudent.

Why be uneasy about it?

Incessantly.

When you shall have expiated your fault

By a little less vanity.

He is more faithful than you.

Unfortunately, no.

No, you are not pretty enough.

That depends on your fortune.

Gluttony.

You will know soon.

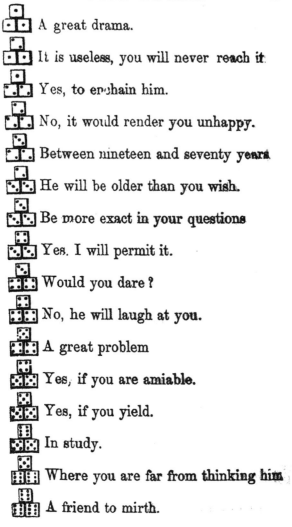

A great drama.

It is useless, you will never reach it

Yes, to enchain him.

No, it would render you unhappy.

Between nineteen and seventy years

He will be older than you wish.

Be more exact in your questions

Yes. I will permit it.

Would you dare ?

No, he will laugh at you.

A great problem

Yes, if you are amiable.

Yes, if you yield.

In study.

Where you are far from thinking him

A friend to mirth.

To forget him.

A child who commits many follies

They think you a little giddy.

Yes, and forever.

By a mortal and reciprocal hatred

You know well it is no.

Yes, but not enough.

Not yet.

His wrongs are very great.

Not to profit by your youth.

No, but honest.

Yes, but your beau will not be so

Yes, but, but, but.

All will soon change.

He should not make mine alone.

Let us go there ; do you not think this?

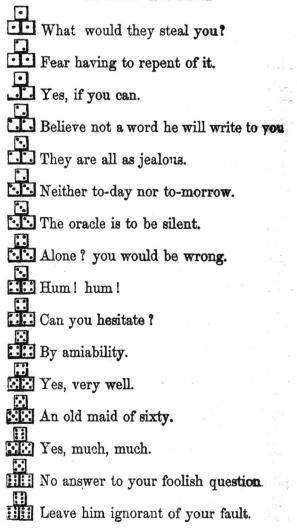

What would they steal **you?**

Fear having to repent of it.

Yes, if you can.

Believe not a word he will write **to you**

They are all as jealous.

Neither to-day nor to-morrow.

The oracle is to be silent.

Alone? you would be **wrong.**

Hum! hum!

Can you hesitate?

By amiability.

Yes, very well.

An old maid of sixty.

Yes, much, much.

No answer to your foolish **question.**

Leave him ignorant of your fault.

It will cost you many tears.

Yes, a sub-lieutenant of dragoons.

Yes, but you will soon scatter it.

She will put many obstacles in the way

Riches for you.

Yes, if you wish him to forsake you.

The blonde is very witty.

Calm your fears, he will be so.

Yes, even high play.

She is not brilliant enough.

That demands reflection.

Yes, if you are reasonable.

To the most frightful misfortunes.

First one, then the other.

That would be a great evil.

The least of your virtues.

HOW TO TELL FORTUNES WITH CARDS.

In order to initiate the reader into the art of telling fortunes from the cards, we must, as a preliminary step, instruct him in the signification of each of the fifty-two cards. Each card has a meaning of its own (although it is varied according to circumstances), as will be shown in the following list.

SIGNIFICATION OF THE CARDS.

The ACE OF HEARTS signifies ardent love: eternal fidelity

The TWO OF HEARTS: a marriage; fidelity in wedlock.

The THREE OF HEARTS: a son born in the course of the year; unity of sentiment.

The FOUR OF HEARTS: the marriage will be blessed with twins; a faithful compact.

The FIVE OF HEARTS: an intimate friend aims at disturbing your domestic happiness, but is foiled.

The SIX OF HEARTS: much domestic happiness; every year a christening; children will receive rich presents from godfathers and godmothers.

The SEVEN OF HEARTS: misfortune threatens the family, but love is proof against all trials.

The EIGHT OF HEARTS: parents and children live together in unity and love; the parents will receive birth-day gifts from their children.

The NINE OF HEARTS: beautiful wedding gifts; a rich dowry; golden ornaments; a necklace; a diamond ring; a gold watch.

The TEN OF HEARTS: blessed with offspring; betrothal; merry weddings in the family; fortunate events occur in the family; joyful news; a great prize; a rich inheritance.

The KNAVE OF HEARTS: bridegroom; a fortunate wooer; the lover will at last soften the heart of his coy charmer; proposals of marriage and consent; you will receive to-morrow a letter containing money.

The QUEEN OF HEARTS: the lady is loved; quiet love; the person will obtain a rich wife; betrothal; marriage; the lady will consent.

The KING OF HEARTS: a man high in station for a husband; a wealthy man will give the bride away, and will likewise furnish the marriage portion. The bridegroom will attain to high honors. On Christmas-day the person will obtain the consent of his or her beloved.

The ACE OF DIAMONDS: happy fortune; a bright and prosperous career; if you trust in God he will not forsake you.

The TWO OF DIAMONDS: terrific forms will appear, but will vanish again; fortune will depart, but will soon return; fortune will at last shower down all her treasures.

The THREE OF DIAMONDS: a husband will seek you when you have learned to cook, to be a good nurse, and to sing; your wife will love you and be faithful to you, if you keep near her and at home; discord with your wedded partner, but finally reconciliation and lasting peace.

The FOUR OF DIAMONDS: you will receive a flower from a loving hand; cherish it faithfully, and it will bring you good fortune and happiness—the first rose that is presented to you will tell you that you are entering the rosy month of love.

The FIVE OF DIAMONDS: parents' death will suddenly change your fate. If a man dies whom you first met on a Friday morning, you will have luck in the lottery; but if a woman in black is the first person you meet on Saturday morning, you will have ill luck in the lottery.

The SIX OF DIAMONDS: unhappy marriage and divorce; separation from an old friend, or from a kind female friend.

The SEVEN OF DIAMONDS: you will live with the constant idea that you will at last be fortunate; with this conceit your life will pass away, and you will at last die happy. You will always hope to win the high prize in the lottery, but you will never win it, until you have been kissed by the greatest lady in the land.

The EIGHT OF DIAMONDS: what you dream on the night between Friday and Saturday, will turn out true. If you do the contrary to that which some one whispers in your ear, you will have good luck. This card also signifies the prosperous course of any business undertaking; a bountiful harvest, and a fruitful marriage.

The NINE OF DIAMONDS: a lady (a gentleman) will love you ardently so long as you have rosy cheeks; when the color fades, her (his) love will fade also.

The TEN OF DIAMONDS: if you wander southward you will there find the happiness you have long sought for; a Southerner will sue for the hand of a young girl; a maiden from the Eastward will fascinate you; a French girl will turn your head, for four-and-twenty hours; a Spaniard will assail your heart with passionate vows of love.

The KNAVE OF DIAMONDS: he (she) who loves you is in the bloom of life; but he (she) will woo (accept) another.

The QUEEN OF DIAMONDS: the first kiss will cause you vexation.

The KING OF DIAMONDS: a joyful bridal; a happy weddingday: endeavors toward a union with a beloved object.

The ACE OF SPADES: if you keep it a secret that you dye your hair (or beard) a certain person will bestow his (her) heart upon you.

The TWO OF SPADES: your heart is set upon money; you will obtain it if you love one person exclusively.

The THREE OF SPADES: victory over an adversary; you will

take a sea voyage, and on ship-board become acquainted with some one who will have great influence upon your happiness; when you reveal your secret to a certain person, the wish will be obtained which you cherish in the most secret corner of your heart.

The FOUR OF SPADES: there is among your circle of acquaintances some one who wishes to be united to you in marriage; consent, and you will not repent it.

The FIVE OF SPADES: you will have sleepless nights from joy. If you drink a glass of water every morning, fasting, you will obtain your wish. Great things are at hand; a time of trial will come, but if you lose not courage, the worst will soon be over.

The SIX OF SPADES: if the person who inquires of the cards imparts what he has upon his mind to the one who is sitting next him, his wish will be fulfilled.

The SEVEN OF SPADES: by means of a lost letter a secret will be revealed, and this will cause much sorrow; an officer will restore the letter, and all will end well.

The EIGHT OF SPADES: the goal which you strive to reach is very near; an event may happen at any moment which will lead you to it at once.

The NINE OF SPADES: temptation to infidelity; the temptation is withstood.

The TEN OF SPADES: good fortune in marriage; ill fortune at the gaming table. You will lose much money at gaming; at last you will give up the practice, and in ripe old age you will be blessed by the birth of a daughter, whom you will name Fortuna.

The KNAVE OF SPADES: treachery and infidelity will lie in wait for you, but you will come victorious out of the trial. Endurance and courage will lead to a speedy marriage.

The QUEEN OF SPADES: if you choose the number you dream of, you will win the highest prize; but you must venture but once, or fortune will forsake you forever.

The KING OF SPADES: you will be drawn into difficulty on account of politics; but you will be so fortunate as to save the life of a person high in station, who will advance you, and you will become prosperous and renowned.

The ACE OF CLUBS: you will become a widower (widow) and will marry a young widow (young man) and have ten children.

The TWO OF CLUBS: if to-morrow morning, about seven o'clock, some one inquires of you concerning any thing whatever, give no answer, and you will escape a great vexation.

The THREE OF CLUBS: by inheritance you will come into possession of a handsome country seat, where you will live for several years, but too extravagantly; when all your money is gone, you will move into a small country town, where you will play a great part to the last.

The FOUR OF CLUBS: you will be slandered and deceived, but

it will turn out for your advantage. At a certain place there is some one waiting for you—let him not wait in vain.

The FIVE OF CLUBS: signifies a person high in office, who is well disposed toward you.

The SIX OF CLUBS: general good luck; for example, a present, an inheritance; success in business; the finding of a treasure.

The SEVEN OF CLUBS: signifies a secret passion, which you will overcome, however, after a struggle of fourteen days.

The EIGHT OF CLUBS: fortunate result of unremitting exertions.

The NINE OF CLUBS: difficulty with the police; suits at law; an inheritance by will.

The TEN OF CLUBS: a long journey by railroad, and great advantages therefrom.

The KNAVE OF CLUBS: signifies jealousy; when it is an unmarried person who inquires of the cards, this jealousy, alas! is well founded

The QUEEN OF CLUBS: an hotel, or place of public resort, where you will make an agreeable acquaintance.

The KING OF CLUBS: vexation, quarrels, strife—a duel—murder and bloodshed, of which, however, the person inquiring of the cards is innocent. This card signifies also an age of eighty years and upward.

HOW TO TELL FORTUNES FROM THE CARDS, ACCORDING TO THE PRECEDING SIGNIFICATION OF THE SINGLE CARDS.

You let the person who inquires of the cards draw several, say seven or eight or more, if you please, unseen, from a complete pack. These drawn cards the person must press to his breast, brow, and mouth, then shuffle them, and lay them with grave earnestness upon the table, so that they form a cross, as in Fig. 1.

We will now give a few examples, showing how, with the aid of some imagination and poetical fancy (due regard being had to the domestic and other circumstances of the person consulting the cards), fortunes may be told in an agreeable and interesting manner.

FIRST EXAMPLE.—Fig. 1.

We will suppose the person inquiring of the cards to be an un-married female.   You may address her in the following manner:

"Lady—the cards speak, but do not be alarmed—I cannot yet hear them quite distinctly; I cannot therefore soothe your anxiety by assuring you that nothing but good fortune will attend you, but in the meanwhile let us hope for the best. See Fig. 1.

"The very first card tells me that there is some one in this company who would be very glad to stand in a nearer relationship to you, and I would advise you to consent—you will not repent of it (*Four of Spades*).   According to the next card, you will, in some hotel, or place of public resort, make an agreeable acquaintance (*Queen of Clubs*), and I can now inform you that the person who loves you is still in the bloom of life, but, alas! I cannot conceal it, he will woo another (*Knave of Diamonds*).   Still, my dear lady, do not be downcast, for the very next card (*Ace of Hearts*) signifies ardent love and eternal fidelity.   It is true, misfortune threatens you and yours, but love is proof against all trials (*Seven of Hearts*). You will be happy, for in a short time you will be united to the one you love, and within a year—do not blush—you will clasp an infant son to your bosom (*Three of Hearts*). Yet no lasting compact can be formed with the powers of Fate; misfortune comes with rapid strides; do not be alarmed, lady, but I must not conceal it from you—the cards declare, clearly and distinctly, that you will be a widow, that you will marry a second time, and ten sweet children will bind you closely to your beloved spouse" (*Ace of Clubs*).

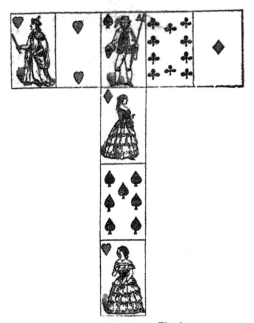

SECOND EXAMPLE.—Fig. 2.

The person inquiring, is this time likewise an unmarried lady.
Having shuffled the cards, you let the lady draw seven or eight
cards, as before. You then say to her: "Lady, your future bridegroom is a man high in station, and a man of wealth will furnish
the marriage portion and lead the bride to the altar (*King of
Hearts*). Fidelity in wedlock will last longer than the bridal fes-
tivities (*Two of Hearts*). True, treachery and infidelity will lie in
wait for you (*Knave of Spades*), but you will come victorious out
of the trial. You will then take a long journey by railroad, from
which great advantages will arise (*Ten of Clubs*), and if you do but
trust in God, you may expect a happy fortune, a bright and prosperous career (*Ace of Diamonds*), yet the first kiss will cause you
vexation (*Queen of Diamonds*). By means of a lost letter a secret
will be revealed, which will occasion you much sorrow (*Seven of
Spades*), but an officer will restore the letter to you, and all will
end well, for henceforth quiet love and happiness will be the fortune of yourself and spouse" (*Queen of Hearts*). See Fig. 2.

THIRD EXAMPLE.—Fig. 3.

The person who in this example consults the cards is a man; after he has drawn the cards, you say: "Sir, the cards speak—all human reasoning is silent; you, as well as all of us, must bow to the inexorable decree of Fate. You will soon have some difficulty with the police, be engaged in suits at law, but you will be, by some one, remembered in a will (*Nine of Clubs*). You will have good fortune in marriage, but ill luck at the gaming table; you will lose much money, but at last will give up gaming, and in ripe old age, you will be blessed with a daughter, whom you will name Fortuna (*Ten of Spades*). You are striving toward a union with a beloved object, a joyful marriage, a happy wedding day is in store for you (*King of Diamonds*). An intimate friend will seek to disturb your domestic peace, but you, watchful over your happiness, will eject him from your house (*Five of Hearts*). If that which you have at this moment upon your mind, you impart to the one who is sitting next to you, your wish will be fulfilled (*Six of Spades*). Perhaps you do not yet know that which I can foretell to you from this card, namely, that to-morrow you will receive a letter containing money (*Knave of Hearts*). I have this yet to say to you: a secret passion agitates you, yet I can give you the assurance that, after a struggle of fourteen days, you will overcome it" (*Seven of Clubs*). See Fig. 3.

THE DREAMER'S DICTIONARY;

I CALL that a dream which proceeds either from the spirit of the hantasy and intellect united together, or by the illustration of the gent intellect above our souls, or by the true revelation of some divine power in a quiet and purified mind; for by this our soul receives true oracles, and abundantly yields prophecies to us; as in dreams we seem both to ask questions, and learn to find them out.

They, therefore, whose intellect, being overwhelmed by too much commerce of the flesh, is in a dead sleep, or funtastic power, or spirit is too dull and unpolished, so that it cannot receive the species and representation which flow from the superior intellect; this man, I say, is altogether unfit for the receiving of dreams and prophesying by them. Therefore, it is necessary that he who would receive true dreams should keep a pure, undisturbed, and imaginative spirit, and so compose it, that it may be made worthy of the knowledge and government by the mind and understanding; for such a spirit is most fit for prophesying, and is a most clear glass of all the images which flow (everywhere) from all things. Therefore, all those who would receive oracles by dreams, and those said oracles true and certain, I would have them to abstain one whole day from meat, and three days from wine or any other strong liquors, and drink nothing but pure water; for to sober and religious minds the pure spirits are adherent, but fly from all those who are drowned in drunkenness and surfeiting. Although impure spirits do very often administer notable secrets to those who are apparently besotted with strong liquors, yet all such communications are to be contemned and avoided.

This is the way whereby we may obtain all sciences and arts whatsoever, whether astrology, occult philosophy, physic, &c., or else suddenly and perfectly with a true illumination of our intellect, although all inferior familiar spirits whatsoever conduce to this effect, and sometimes also evil spirits sensibly inform us, intrinsically.

I shall now proceed to treat you with the common interpretations of dreams in the following alphabetical order:

ACQUAINTANCE. To dream that you fight with them, signifies distraction, especially if the person so dreaming be sick. 42, 6.

AGUE. To dream that you have one, and are very cold, shows an inclination to strong drink, wine, spices, and other hot things. 39, 6, 1.

AIR. To dream that you see it clear and serene, shows you

shall be beloved and esteemed by all people, and that those who are your enemies and envy you, shall be reconciled to you. It also denotes the discovery of lost goods, or things that have been stolen. If the person so dreaming be at law, he shall overthrow his adversary; and if he designs a voyage or journey, he shall be successful therein. And, in short, all good things are denoted by a clear and serene air. But to dream that the air is cloudy, dark, and troubled, denotes to the dreamer sadness, grief, sickness, melancholy, loss of goods, hindrance of business, and is in all things the reverse of dreaming what we have before mentioned of a clear and serene air. But for a man to dream that the air is very calm and without winds or storms, denotes his life to be peaceable, and that he shall be acceptable to all company; and that whatever business, journey by land, or voyage by sea he undertakes, shall prosper and succeed according to his wishes. 12, 9.

ALMONDS. *See Fruit.*

ALMS. To dream that they are begged of you, and you deny to give them, shows want and misery to the dreamer; but to dream that you give them freely is a sign of great joy and of long life to the dreamer. 11, 13, 4.

ANCHOR. To dream you see one, signifies great assurance and certain hope. 47, 36.

ANGER. To dream that you have been provoked to anger, shows that you have many powerful enemies. 44, 16.

ANTS. To dream of them, betokens an earthly, covetous mind; and, as they live under the earth, to dream often of them, shows the dreamer not to be long lived. To see ants with wings, shows a dangerous voyage, or other ill accident. To dream you see common ants, which are diligent and industrious in providing their food, is good for ploughmen and farmers, because they signify fertility; for where there is no grain you will find no ants. To such as live upon the public, and reap profits by many, they are very good; and to such as are sick, if they dream they come near the body; for they are industrious and cease not to labor, which is proper to such as live; but if they dream that ants range about their bodies, it is a token of death; because they are inhabitants of earth, and are cold and black. 7, 49, 20.

APPAREL. To dream that your apparel is proper, and suited to the season of the year, denotes prosperity and happiness; or that your apparel is made of linen and fine wool, if in the summer is good; but in the winter it is better to dream your apparel is new, and made of strong cloth. To dream of white apparel is good only to priests, because it belongs to them in the administration of their sacred function; but to others it signifies trouble; to mechanics it signifies want of business; to the sick, white apparel denotes death; but that which is black, their recovery. To be apparelled in a garment of divers colors, or of scarlet, is good for priests and players; but to others it denotes dangers, troubles, and a discovery of such things as ought to be concealed. And unto the sick, the dreaming of their being so apparelled, shows that they shall be much troubled with a redundancy of humors. For rich men and servants to be arrayed in scarlet robes, is a signification of honor, dignity, and liberty. But such a dream brings death to the sick, and an increase of poverty to the poor, and to many captivity. To be apparelled in a robe dyed in scarlet, signifies hurts to some, and agues to others. As to women's apparel: to dream of a woman's gown, it is good only to single persons, and such as come to act their parts upon stages; for married men after such dreams have lost their wives, or fallen into great sickness, because those who wear such garments are effeminate persons. Notwithstanding which, to dream of gowns of divers colors, or of women's gowns, is not at all bad, when you dream likewise that it is upon the account of great rejoicing, or of public assemblies. To dream you are apparelled in a gown of the fashion of some strange nation, shows such a one good luck among strangers, if they design to go among them. To dream of having a delicate and sumptuous gown, is good both to rich and poor; for, to the first, their present prosperity shall continue, and to the other, their goods shall increase. Gowns that are torn show hurt and hindrance of affairs. 17, 20.

APPLES. To dream you see apple-trees, and eat sweet and ripe apples, denotes joy, pleasure, and recreation, especially to virgins; but sour apples signify contention and sedition. 4, 11, 44.

APRICOTS. *See Fruit.*

ASS. The ass in dreams denotes a good servant or slave, that is profitable to his master: it also indicates a foolish and ignorant person. To dream you see an ass, is a sign of malice. To see an ass sitting on his crupper, denotes laboriousness. To dream you hear an ass bray, shows you shall meet with some loss. To dream of asses bearing charge, strong and obedient, is good for friendship and company, and signifies the wife's companion or friend being not proud above their estate, or fierce, but gentle and very obedient; they are also good in affairs and enterprises. To see an ass run, denotes misfortune, especially to a man that is sick, 62, 18, 20.

AUTHORITY. It is good always for a rich man to think or dream he is in authority. 21.

BACK. To dream you see your back, betokens some unhappiness; for the back and all the hinder parts signify old age. To dream a man's back is broken, hurt, or scabby, shows his enemies will get the better of him, and that he will be scoffed at. To dream of the back-bone, indicates health and joy, and that he will take delight in his wife and children. 2, 19, 42.

BAGPIPES. To dream that you play upon them, denotes trouble, contention, and being overthrown at law. 20, 1.

BANQUETS. To dream of banquets is very good and prosperous, and promises great preferment. 11.

BARLEY-BREAD. To dream of eating barley-bread, betokens health and comfort. 1, 15.

BARN. To dream you see a barn stored with corn, shows that you shall marry a rich wife, overthrow your adversary at law, inherit land, or grow rich by trading. 4, 75.

BASIN. To dream of a basin, indicates a good maid; and to dream you eat or drink therein, shows you have a love to the servant-maid. For a man to see himself in a basin, as in a glass, denotes he shall have children by a servant-maid. 2, 13, 69.

BATH. To dream one sees a bath, is a sign of affliction or grief. If a person dreams he goes into, or sees himself in a bath, and that he finds it too hot, he will be troubled and afflicted by those that belong to his family. If one dreams he has only pulled off his clothes, without going into the bath, he will have some disturbance, but of no long continuance. If one dreams he goes into an extremely cold bath, the same signification is to be given of it as when it is too hot. But if it be temperate, and as it ought to be, it is a good dream, presaging prosperity, joy, and health. 20, 31.

BAY-TREE. To dream of the bay-tree, denotes a rich and fair wife; and also ill success of affairs, because it is bitter; but it is good for physicians, poets, and divines to dream of it. 17.

BEANS. To dream you are eating beans, always betokens trouble and dissensions. 72, 18, 11.

BEAR. To dream that you have seen a bear denotes you have a rich, puissant, inexpert, but cruel and audacious enemy. 68.

BEES. To dream of bees is good and bad: good, if they sting not, but bad, if they sting the party dreaming, for then the bees do signify enemies; and therefore to dream that bees fly about your ears, shows your being beset with many enemies; but if you beat them off, without being stung by them, it is a sign of victory, and of your overcoming them. To dream of seeing bees, indicates profit to country people, and trouble to the rich; yet to dream that they make honey in any part of the house or tenement, is a sign of dignity, eloquence, and good success in business. To take bees, shows profit and gain, by reason of their honey and wax. 17, 62, 4.

BEHEADING. To dream that one is beheaded, and that the head is separated from the body, denotes liberty to prisoners, health to the sick, comfort to those in distress; to creditors, payment of debts. To princes, good fortune, and that their cares and fears will be turned into joy and confidence in their subjects. If one dreams that a person of his acquaintance beheads him, he will share with him in his pleasures and honors. If any one dreams that a young child, who has not yet attained the age of his youth, hath cut off his head, if the dreamer be sick, he will not live long; if in health, he will get honor. If a woman with child dream thus, she will bring forth a male child, and her husband will die suddenly; for he is her head. To dream that you see one beheaded, betokens sickness.   74, 19, 10.

BELLY. To dream one's belly is bigger and fuller than ordinary, shows his family and estate will increase proportionably, according to the greatness of his belly. If one dreams his belly is grown lean and shrunk up, he will be joyfully delivered from some bad accident. If any one dreams that his belly is swelled, and yet notwithstanding empty, he will become poor, though he be rich in the esteem of many people in the world.   24, 77.

BIRDS. To dream you see many birds, denotes assemblies and suits at law. To dream of catching birds by lime twigs, or with nets, shows the entrapping or ensnaring of enemies by deceitful means. To dream of great birds, is better for the rich than the poor. To dream of little birds, the contrary. To dream that you hear little birds chirp is a good sign. To see birds fighting betokens adversity. To see birds fly over your head, shows prejudice by enemies. To see blackbirds, denotes trouble. To hear birds sing, is joy and delight.   14, 77.

BIRDS-NESTS. To dream you find one is a good sign. To dream you find one without either eggs or birds, shows you will meet with a great disappointment.   64.

BIRDING. To dream you catch birds, is a sign of profit and pleasure.

BLIND. To dream of being blind, shows a man shall be admonished to foresee his errors and avoid them, especially in love affairs. This dream also threatens the dreamer with want of money—when a man at noon-day cannot see a penny in his purse, which is a common kind of blindness.   66.

BLOOD. To dream you vomit much blood, and of a good color is good for him that is poor, for he shall get store of money. It is also very good for him who hath no children, and whose kindred are in a strange country: the first shall see a child of his own; the other, his kindred returning home. To dream of carrying blood, is not good for them that desire to be hidden. To dream you vomit corrupt blood, is sickness to all. To cast a little blood in spitting, foretells sedition, as some have known by experience. 11, 19.

BLOWING THE FIRE. To dream of blowing the fire, denotes, to the rich, servitude; to the poor, profit. To dream of stirring up and blowing the fire, denotes also the stirring up of wrath, and that old quarrels, that have long lain dormant, shall be revived.   27.

BOAT. To dream you are in a boat upon a river, lake, or pond of clear water, is very good, and indicates joy, prosperity, and good success in affairs. If a man dream that he is walking in a boat, and recreating himself without fear, he will have comfort and success in his affairs: but if the water be rough and tempestuous, it falleth out contrary. 71, 10.

BRASS. *See Metals.*

BREAD. To dream of eating such bread as is usual, or as the person dreaming is accustomed to, is good: but to dream of eating unusual bread is bad: and therefore for the poor to dream they eat white bread, denotes sickness, and for the rich to dream they eat brown bread, shows they shall meet with some obstructions in their affairs. To dream of barley-bread, is good for all, for it signifies health and content. 1, 15.

BREWING AND BAKING. To dream of brewing and baking, is a sign of an ill housewife, who lies dreaming in bed when she should be at work and doing her business. 31.

BRIDGE. For one to dream that he goes over a broken bridge, betokens fear; and to dream you fall upon a bridge, is a sign of obstruction in business. 56, 2.

BROTH. To dream of eating broth, is a good sign, and indicates profit or gain. 32, 9.

BRETHREN. To dream that you discourse with your brethren, betokens vexations; because our brethren bring us nothing when they are born, but diminish our inheritance and succession, and are the cause that those things which would be all our own, are divided into many parts between them and us. Timocrates dreamed that he buried, or caused to be interred, one of his brothers, departed, and a little while after, one of his chief adversaries died. To dream of the death of our brethren, signifieth, not only the loss of our enemies, but also deliverance or acquittance from some loss or hurt which attended us, and whereof we stood in fear; as it happened to Diocles, the grammarian, who sustained no loss of money, whereof he stood in doubt, and was afraid because he dreamed before that he saw his brother dead. 24, 8.

BURIED ALIVE. For a man to dream he is buried alive, shows he is in danger of being unhappy and unfortunate during his life. 11, 14.

BUSINESS. To dream you manage business of great concernment shows you will meet obstructions. 41.

CAGE. To dream that a maid lets a bird out of a cage, is a sign she will not long keep her honor, but as soon as she can, will part with it. 36, 5.

CANDLE. To dream one sees a candle extinguished, denotes sadness, sickness, and poverty. When one dreams he sees a shining lighted candle, it is a good sign to the sick, denoting recovery and health: and if he that dreams be unmarried, it shows he will speedily marry, have success, and prosper in his undertakings. To dream that you make candles, is a sign of rejoicing. To dream that you see candles not lighted, shows you shall have a reward for something you have done. 21, 67, 46.

CANNON. *See Fire-arms.*

CRANBERRIES. *See Fruit.*

CAPON. To dream that a capon crows, indicates sadness and trouble. 15.

CARDS. Playing at cards, tables, or any other game in a dream, shows the party shall be very fortunate: and tables allude unto love, for love is the table, fancy the point that stands open; and he that dreams much of table playing, shall be a great gamester, as well with Joan as my lady. 76, 17.

CARROTS. To dream of carrots, denotes profit; and strength to them who are at law for an inheritance: for we pluck them out of the ground with their heads, branches, strings, and veins. 10, 35.

CART. To dream of being tied in a cart, to draw like a horse or an ox, denotes servitude and pain to everybody, how rich and mighty soever they be. To dream that you are carried in your cart or coach, to be drawn by men, signifies to have might and authority over many, and to have children of good behavior. As for travellers, it is to go slowly, but surely, when they have such a dream. 6, 5, 17.

CATTLE. To dream of keeping cattle, portends disgrace and loss to the rich, but profit to the poor. Also, to dream of fat cattle, shows a fruitful year, but lean cattle denote scarcity. 6, 11, 66.

CERBERUS. To dream you see the dog Cerberus, whom the poets feign to be the porter of hell, signifies sin, which bites every one; and arrests by sergeants, who are men void of pity, and bring all they lay hold of to misery. 54.

CHARIOT. To dream of guiding a chariot drawn by wolves, leopards, dogs, tigers, or such like beasts, is only good to those who have great enemies. To dream of being drawn in a chariot by men, is only good to those that desire to command and be obeyed; to others it denotes loss and discredit. 45.

CHEESE. To dream you eat cheese, is a sign of profit and gain. 65, 3.

CHERRIES. *See Fruit.*

CHILDREN. To dream that a man sees two or three children born, shows he shall have cause of joy, and meet with good success in his business. When one dreams that he hath many small children, and that they seem to him to run about the house, and yet notwithstanding he hath none, it signifies it will be very difficult for him ever to have any, besides which, he that so dreams, will have many cares and obstructions in his affairs. If any one dreams he sees himself wrapped in clothes, in fashion of little children, and to suck some woman's breast which he knoweth, it argues long sickness, if he have not his wife at that time with child; but if his wife hath such a dream, he shall have a daughter. And here note, that among little children, it is better to dream that you see boys than girls. To dream of any thing to befall little children, which is not proper to their age, is not good; as to dream that boys have beards and gray hairs, and that little girls should be married and have children, which betokens to them death. 5, 56.

CLOAK. To dream that one has lost his cloak, is good if it be old, for thereby is signified, that the party so dreaming shall have a new one; but if he dream of finding it again, then he shall have no change, but shall keep the old one still. 32.

CLOTHES. If a man dream he has a new suit of clothes, it is a sign of honor. To dream that you see your clothes burned, denotes loss and damage. To dream that you see yourself in black clothes, signifies joy. To dream that you take your clothes to put them on, denotes loss. If a man or woman dream they are meanly clothed, it betokens trouble and sadness. If one dreams his clothes are dirty, that he hath bad clothes, tattered and much worn, it means shame. To dream your clothes are embroidered all over with gold, or any other kind of embroidery, signifies joy and honor. 24.

CLOUDS. To dream of white clouds, is a sign of prosperity; clouds mounting high from the earth, denote voyages, and return of the absent, and revealing of secrets. Clouds red and inflamed, show an ill issue of affairs; to dream of smoky, dark, or obscure clouds, shows an ill time, or anger. 47, 8.

COACH. To dream of riding in a coach, shows that the party so dreaming shall love idleness, is given to pride, and shall die a beggar. To dream of coming out of a coach, denotes being degraded from great honor, and coming into disgrace upon a criminal account. 41.

COAL-PITS. To dream of being at the bottom of coal-pits, indicates matching with a widow; for he that marries her must be a continual drudge, and yet shall never sound the depth of her policies. 12.

COOK. To dream you see a cook in the house, is good to those who would marry, for marriages are not good without a cook; it is also good for the poor, for they shall have goods, and ability to keep a good and long table; to the sick it is inflammation, heat, and tears. 6, 34.

COPPER. (See Metals.)

COUNTENANCE. To dream you see a comely countenance unlike your own, betokens honor. 28.

CRANBERRIES. (See Fruit.)

CUCUMBERS. To dream of eating cucumbers, denotes vain hopes, but to the sick it is a prognostic of recovery. 16, 8.

CURRANTS. (See Fruit.)

DAIRY. To dream of being in a dairy, showeth the dreamer to be of a milksop nature. 71, 2.

DANCING. For a man to dream that he sees himself dance alone, or in the presence of his household, also to see his wife, children, or either of his parents dance, is good; for it shows abundance of mirth; but to him that is sick, or hath any disease about him, it is evil. 55, 27.

DARK. To dream of being in the dark, and that he cannot find his way out of the room, or so that he loses his way in riding, or in going up a high pair of stairs, denotes that the party so dreaming shall be blinded with some passion, and much troubled. 4, 16.

DATES. (*See Fruit.*)

DEAD MAN. To dream that you see a dead man, signifieth that he that dreams will be subject to the same passions and fortune as the party deceased had when alive, if he knew him. 61.

DEAD. To dream of talking with dead folks, is a good auspicious dream; it shows great courage, and a very clear conscience. To dream a man is dead, who is alive and in health, denotes great trouble and being overthrown at law. 61, 4.

DEATH. To dream of death, signifies a wedding; for death and marriage represent one another. For the sick to dream they are married, or that they celebrate their weddings, is a sign of death, and signifies separation from her or his companions, friends, or parents; for the dead keep not company with the living. 61, 4.

DEBT. To dream of debt, we are to take notice that the debtor and the creditor represent life; wherefore, to the sick, the creditor urging and constraining is great danger and receiving of death; for we owe a life to nature, our universal mother, which she makes us restore and pay. 18, 64.

DESCENDING INTO HELL. To dream that you are descending into hell, and return thence, signifies to those that are great and rich, misfortunes; but it is a good sign to the poor and weak. 17.

DEVIL. To dream that one has seen the devil, and that he is tormented, or otherwise much terrified, is a sign the dreamer is in danger of being checked and punished by his sovereign prince, or some magistrate. 61, 18.

DIGGING. To dream you are digging, is very good; but if you dream that your spades or digging tools seem to be lost, it portends loss of labor, dearth of corn, and ill harvest weather. 14, 71.

DITCHES. To dream you see great ditches or precipices, and that you fall into them, is a sign that he who dreams will suffer much injury and hazard by his person, and his goods be in danger by fire. To dream you go over a ditch by a small plank, means much deceit by lawyers. 73, 8.

DOGS. When we dream of such dogs as belong to us, it signifies fidelity, courage and affection; but if we dream of those which belong to strangers, it means infamous enemies. To dream that a dog barks and tears our garments, betokens some enemy of mean condition slanders us,.or endeavors to deprive us of our live-lihood. 17, 61.

DRAGON. To dream you see a dragon, is a sign you shall see some great lord your master, or a magistrate; it implies also riches and treasure. 19.

DRINKING. To dream you are drinking, when you are very dry, is an assured sign of sickness, especially if your dream be near the break of day, and the dreamer be of a sanguine complexion, and lying on the left side. 67.

EAGLE. To dream you see an eagle in some high place, is a good sign to those who undertake any weighty business, and es-pecially to soldiers. If one dreams that an eagle lights upon his head, it betokens death to the dreamer. 48.

EARTH. If a man dreams that he hath good lands, or earth well inclosed, bestowed upon him, with pleasant pastures, he will have a handsome wife. If you dream you see the earth black, that implies sorrow, melancholy, and the weakness of the brain. 17.

EARTH-WORMS. Dreaming of earth-worms betokens secret enemies, that endeavor to ruin and destroy us. 14.

ECLIPSE. For one to dream that he sees the sun in eclipse, means the loss of his father; but if he sees the moon eclipsed in his dream, it betokeneth the death of his mother; but if the party dreaming have neither father nor mother, then the death of the next nearest relation. 8.

ELEPHANT. To dream one sees an elephant, signifies the party shall be rich; for if one dreams he is carried on an elephant, he shall enjoy the estate of some great prince or lord; and if one dreams that he gives an elephant any thing to eat or drink, it is a sign he shall wait upon some great lord to his advantage. 33.

EVIL SPIRITS. Dreaming that evil spirits shall obstruct thy doing good, under a show of devotion, shows thou wilt be obstruct-ed in thy affairs by a hypocrite. And if thou dreamest that thou seest hideous physiognomies, things more than common shall be revealed to thee. 5.

EYEBROWS. Dreaming the eyebrows are hairy, and of a good grace, is good, especially to women. But the eyebrows naked and without hair, implies she will be afraid to marry. But if either man or woman dream their eyebrows are more comely and large than they used to be, it is a sign they will do feats in the matri-monial way. 18.

EYES. If any one dream he hath lost his eyes, it shows he will violate his word, or else that he or some of his children are in danger of death, or that he will never more see his friends again. 66, 49, 78.

FACE. To dream you see a fresh, taking, smiling face and countenance, is a sign of friendship and joy. Dreaming you see a meagre, pale face, is a sign of trouble, poverty, and dearth. Dreaming one washes his face, implies repentance for sin; a black face is a sign of long life. 5, 11, 55.

FAIRS. To dream of going to fairs, threatens the person so dreaming with having his pocket picked, which is usually done in those places. 31, 15.

FALL. Dreaming you had a fall from a tree, been scratched by thorns, or otherwise prejudiced, signifies you shall lose your office, and be out of favor with grandees. 65, 70.

FATHER-IN-LAW. To dream one sees his father-in-law, either dead or alive, is ill, especially if he dreams that he uses violence or threatening. And to dream that he uses gentle speech and good entertainment, implies vain hopes and deceit. 16.

FEET. To dream that a man's feet are cut off, betokens damage. Dreaming one hath a wooden leg, implies the alteration of your condition from good to bad, and from bad to worse. 51.

FIELDS. Dreaming of fields and pleasant places, shows a man that he will marry a discreet, chaste, and beautiful wife, and that she will bear him handsome children. And to women it betokens a loving and prudent husband. 16, 72, 6.

FIGHTING. To dream of fighting, signifies opposition and contention; and if the party dreams he is wounded in fighting, it implies loss of reputation and disgrace. 44, 78.

FINGERS. Dreaming you cut your fingers, or see them cut by another, betokens damage. To dream you lose some or all of your fingers, implies either the hurt or loss of servants. To scriveners, orators, and attorneys it is a sign they shall want employment; to debtors, that they shall pay more than they owe · to usurers, loss by interest. 1, 2.

FIRE. When a man dreams of fire, or that he sees fire, it means the issue of his choler; and commonly they that dream of fire are active and furious; if a man dreams he is burnt by fire, a violent fever is prognosticated thereby. When a man dreams that his bed is on fire, and that he perished, it betokens damage, sickness, or death to his wife; and if the wife dream it, the same will happen to her husband. If one dream that the kitchen is on fire, that denotes death to his cook. 26.

FIRE-ARMS. To dream of fire-arms, denotes uproar, quarrels, sedition. 16, 21, 57.

FISH. If any one dreams he sees or catches large fish, it is a sign of profit. Dreaming you see fish of divers colors, means to the sick, poison; and to those in health, injuries, contention, and grief. A woman with child, that dreams she is delivered of a fish, shall (according to the opinion of the ancients) be delivered of a dead child. 14, 71.

FLATTERY. To dream one is pleasant, and easily endures flattery, is not good; especially if one of our familiars, for it signifies to be betrayed by him. 41.

FLESH. If any one dreams he has increased in flesh, he will

gain wealth; on the contrary, if you dream you have got thin, you will grow poor. If you dream your flesh is spotted or black, you will prove deceitful. 65.

FLOWERS. If you dream of holding or smelling odoriferous flowers in their season, it means joy; on the contrary, to dream that you see or smell flowers out of season, if they be white, it denotes obstruction in business, and bad success. 14, 7, 43.

FLYING. Flying in the air, is prosperity; very high, honor, low, riches. 35.

FOG. To see a fog, is lucky; but to see it disappear, is unlucky. 21.

FORTUNE TELLING. To dream you tell another's fortune, denotes that some person will occasion you much trouble. 76, 8, 4.

FORTUNE. To dream you make a sudden fortune, is a bad omen; to a tradesman, it forebodes heavy losses; to the lover, it denotes crosses. 76, 8, 4.

FRUIT. To dream of fruit, has different interpretations, according to the fruit you dream of. To enable our readers more readily to discover the meaning of their dreams, we have arranged the fruits alphabetically, with their explanations. 32.

ALMONDS foretell deceit in love, and great privation in marriage. 73, 18, 10.

APPLES betoken faithfulness in love, and long life. 4, 11, 44.

APRICOTS denote health and prosperity to the married; to the single, marriage. 22, 5, 64.

BLACK CURRANTS denote happiness in life, and constancy in love. 12, 5, 60.

CHERRIES are unfavorable omens; they portend vexation and trouble in marriage, and inconstancy in love. 14, 54.

DEWBERRIES. To dream you are picking them, denotes to lovers speedy marriage, but to the married, great losses. 11.

CRANBERRIES portend a faithful partner and many children. 7.

DATES denote many enemies, and you will receive much injury by a person you little expect. 6, 44.

ELDERBERRIES, riches; to the single, marriage. 30, 33.

FIGS denote prosperity; to the lover, success. 6, 29.

FILBERTS forebode much trouble and danger. 76.

GOOSEBERRIES indicate many children, and your undertakings will prosper. 19, 8.

GRAPES foretell a cheerful husband to the maiden; happiness in marriage. 70.

LEMONS denote contention in your family; constancy in love, and a partner of a happy temper. 22.

MULBERRIES denote to the maiden a happy marriage; to the married, affection and constancy. 64, 70, 3.

NUTS denote riches and happiness; to the lover, success; if

you are gathering them, it is a good omen; but if you crack them, unfavorable. 48, 6.

ORANGES are very bad omens; they foretell losses in trade; attacks from thieves; and unfaithfulness in your partner. 3, 12, 36.

PEACHES are favorable to the dreamer. If you are in love, your love is returned. 17, 1, 9.

PEARS portend elevation in life, riches, honors, and constancy in love. If a woman with child dream of them, she will have a daughter. 33.

PLUMS augur little good to the dreamer; to dream you are picking them, denotes that your partner is deceitful; if eating them, you will surely meet with some heavy affliction. 36, 14, 77.

RASPBERRIES foretell success in your undertakings, happiness in marriage, and fidelity in your sweetheart. 3, 66.

RED CURRANTS denote happiness in life, and success in love. 12, 5, 60.

STRAWBERRIES denote a happy marriage. 39, 78.

WHITE CURRANTS portend that your partner will fall into difficulties, and will have a long illness. 12, 5, 60.

FUNERAL. To dream one goes to a funeral of a friend, is a good sign; the dreamer shall have money, or marry a fortune. 18, 1.

GARDEN. To dream of walking in a garden, and gathering flowers, shows the person is given to pride and to have high thoughts of herself. If a man dream of seeing fair gardens, he will marry a chaste and beautiful wife. 31, 17.

GEESE. If you dream of the cackling of geese, you will have an increase of business, and much profit. 15, 69.

GIANT. If you dream of seeing a giant, or a large-sized man, it is a good sign. 31, 4.

GIBBET. To dream you see a person hanging on a gibbet, is a sign of damage and great affliction. 45.

GIRDLE. Dreaming you are girt with a girdle, means labor and pains. If you dream you have a new girdle it means honor. 20.

GLASS. If one dreams that he hath a glass given him full of water, he shall be married speedily, and his wife shall have children But if the glass is cracked, he must look sharp after his wife's chastity. 11, 64.

GOAT. To dream of goats, is a sign of wealth and plenty. 64, 34.

GOD. Dreaming that we worship God, is good. To dream of receiving pure gifts from Him, shows good health. 1.

GOLD. (*See Metals.*)

GOOSEBERRIES. (*See Fruit.*)

GRAIN. If you dream of seeing and gathering grain, it denotes prosperity; if you dream of eating it in pottage, it is bad. 69.

GRAVE. If you dream of being put into a grave and buried, it presageth you shall die in a mean condition. 23.

GROVES. Dreaming you have land and groves adjoining, denotes you will marry well, and be blessed with children. 31.

GROUND. Dreaming you fall upon the ground, denotes dishonor, shame, and scandal. 27.

GUNS. (*See Fire-arms.*)

HAIL. To dream of hail, denotes sorrow and trouble. 21, 72.

HAIR. For a man to dream his hair is long, like a woman's, denotes cowardice and effeminacy, and that the person dreaming will be deceived by a woman. If you dream you see a woman without hair, famine and sickness will ensue. If you see a man bald and without hair, it signifies the contrary. If you dream you cannot pass the comb through your hair, and cannot disentangle it, it portends great trouble and law-suits. 42.

HATRED. Dreaming of hatred, or being hated, whether of friends or enemies, is an ill omen. 44.

HEAD. To dream you have a great head, or a head bigger than ordinary, and very highly raised, denotes dignity. If you dream of your head being cut off by robbers and murderers, that indicates loss of children, relations, estate, or wife; and to a wife so dreaming, the loss of her husband. 65, 9.

HEAVEN. Dreaming of heaven, and that you ascend up thither, is an indication of grandeur and glory. 27.

HEN. If you dream you hear hens cackle, or that you catch them, it denotes joy, and an increase of property, and success in business. Dreaming you see a hen with her chickens, means loss and damage. If you see a hen lay eggs, that denotes gain. 19.

HILLS. To dream you are travelling over hills, and wading through great difficulties, and meet with assistance in the way, means that you shall have good counsel, and overcome all your troubles. 1, 46, 18.

HORNS. If you dream of having horns on your head, it denotes grandeur. If you see a man with horns on his head, he is in danger of loss of his person and estate. 9, 18, 36.

HORSES. If you dream of a horse, it is a good sign: or if one dreams he mounts a horse, it is a happy omen. To dream you are riding on a tired horse, shows one shall be desperately in love. 2, 11, 22.

HOUSE. To dream one builds a house, denotes comfort. Dreaming of building houses, wearing fine clothes, and talking with ladies, is a sign that the parties will suddenly marry. 47, 66.

HUSBANDRY. If you dream of a plough, it is good for marriages. To dream of the yoke, is good, but not for servants. 76, 44.

ICE—denotes a good harvest to husbandmen; and to merchants, and to other men of employment, it betokens hindrance in their negotiations and voyages. 4, 28.

IMAGES. Dreaming you make images of men, denotes you will shortly be married and have many children, and very like yourselves. 69.

INNKEEPER. If you dream of an innkeeper, it betokens death to the sick. The inn means the same as the innkeeper. 43.

IRON. For one to dream he is hurt with iron, is a sign he shall receive some damage. (*See Metals.*)

ILL-FAVOREDLY. To dream that you are ill-favoredly attired, is ill, and signifies abundance of mocking and flouting, with ill issue of affairs. This dream is good only to players. 46, 33.

JOLLITY. Dreaming of jollity, feasts, and merrymakings, is a good and prosperous dream, and promiseth great preferment. 20.

KEYS. To dream you lose your keys, denotes anger. But to dream you have a bunch of keys, and that you give them to those that desire them of you, shows goodness to the poor. A key seen in a dream, to him that would marry, denotes he shall have a handsome wife and a maid. 41, 8.

KING. Dreaming you discourse with a king, implies honor. 4, 14.

KNEES. Dreaming your knees are strong and sturdy, shows health and strength to go through your various avocations; but to dream they are weak, the contrary. If a man dreams that by the strength of his knees he can run swiftly, he shall be happy in all his undertakings. If it be a woman, she will be ready and willing to obey her husband, and be careful to govern her family. 22, 37, 35.

KNIFE. To dream you bestow a knife upon any one, denotes injustice and contention. 33, 9.

LABOR. Dreaming that a woman is in labor, and that she bringeth forth a dead child, showeth that the person shall labor for that which he shall never bring to pass. But if she bring forth a living child, it shows that the parties so dreaming shall succeed in their enterprises. 27, 9.

LAND. If a man dream he has good lands, well enclosed, he shall have a handsome wife. If he dreams that the lands have gardens, fountains, pleasant groves, and orchards, he will marry a discreet, chaste, and beautiful wife, and have children. 34, 61, 18.

LAUREL. If you dream you see a laurel-tree, it denotes victory and pleasure; and, if you be married, it betokens inheritance of possessions. Dreaming you see or smell laurel, if it be a married woman, she shall bear children; if a maid, she will be suddenly married. 71, 13, 1.

LEAD. (*See Metals.*)

LEMONS. (*See Fruit.*)

LETTERS. Dreaming that you learn letters, is good to the ignorant; but to one that has learned his letters it is not good. 28, 54, 1.

MAD. For a man to dream he is mad, and is guilty of ex-

travagancies, he shall be long-lived, and become of great consequence. 4.

MALLOWS. If you dream of eating mallows, it denotes ex-
emption from trouble, and despatch of business. 25.

MANURE. Dreaming that you manure and cultivate the
earth, is a sign of melancholy to those who are in good condition;
but to laborers it signifies gain and a plentiful crop. 9.

MARJORAM. Dreaming that you smell marjoram denotes
trouble, labor, and sadness. 28.

MARRIAGE. To dream that you do the act of marriage, denotes danger. Marriage, or the wedding of a woman, is a token
of the death of some friend; and for a man to dream that he is
newly married, and that he hath had to do with his new wife, it
denotes some evil accident will befall him. 2, 78, 42.

MARSHES. Dreaming of marshes, is good only for shepherds:
to all others they are a sign of hindrance of business. 64.

MARTYR. If one dreams that he dies for religion, the person
will arrive at a great point of honor; and it denotes that his
soul will be happy hereafter. 45.

MEASLES. If any one dreams he hath the measles, it denotes
he shall gain wealth, but it shall be with infamy. 33, 4.

MELONS. Dreaming of melons, is to sick persons a prognostic
of recovery, by reason of their juicy substance 46.

METALS. To dream of metals has different significations and
interpretations, according to the metal you dream of. To enable
our readers to more readily discover the meaning of their dreams,
we subjoin a list of the metals with their explanations.

BRASS. To dream that you see a brass ornament, is a sign
your sweetheart will be false to you. To see any one working in
brass, or cleaning that metal, is a sign you will hear of the death
of a distant relative who will leave you a legacy. 43, 11.

COPPER. To dream of copper, signifies that your sweetheart is
deceitful and loves another, it also shows secret enemies. 54, 8, 40.

GOLD. To dream of receiving gold is a good sign, and shows
you will be successful in all your undertakings. To dream you
pay gold, betokens increase of friends. 49, 7.

IRON. For one to dream that he is hurt with iron, signifies that
he shall receive some damage. 44, 5.

LEAD. To dream of lead denotes sickness, but to dream of
leaden bullets, good news. If you dream you are wounded by
leaden bullet, it is a sign you will be successful in love. 49, 50.

QUICKSILVER. To dream of this metal, is a sign your friends
will all be false to you; it is also a sign of losses in property.
49, 19.

SILVER. To dream that you are presented with spoons, or any
silver plate for household use, foretells that you or some near relative, will shortly marry; if you dream of buying these articles,
it is a sign of poverty. To dream of silver dollars, or bars of sil-

ver, used in commerce, is a sign that you will gain money either by a legacy or speculation. 49, 6.

STEEL. To break a piece in a dream, shows that you will overcome your enemies; if you only touch it, your position in life is secure; if you try to bend it, and cannot, you will meet with many serious accidents. 41, 50.

TIN. To dream of tin, is a good omen, and signifies you will marry a rich wife, and make money at business. 41, 8.

ZINC. To dream of this metal, denotes happiness and prosperity to the dreamer. To lovers, it is a sign of success in love affairs. 48.

MILK. To dream you drink milk, is an extraordinary good sign; and to dream you see breasts full of milk, denotes gain. 45, 60.

MOLE. Dreaming of a mole, denotes a man blind by inconvenience and labor in vain, and also that he who would be secret shall be disclosed by himself. 35.

MONKEYS. Dreaming of monkeys, shows you have malicious, strange, and secret enemies. 17, 6.

MOON. If any one dream that he sees the moon shine, it shows that his wife loves him extremely well; it also implies the getting of silver; for, as the sun represents gold, so the moon doth silver. Dreaming you see the moon darkened, denotes the death or sickness of your wife, mother, sister, or daughter; loss of money, or danger in a voyage or journey, especially if it be by water; or else it denotes a distemper in the brain or eyes. To dream you see the moon darkened, and grow clear and bright again, implies gain to the woman that dreams, and to the man joy and prosperity; but to dream that you see the moon clear, and afterward cloudy, presageth the contrary. To dream you see the moon in the form of a full white face, implies to the virgin, speedy marriage; to the married woman, that she will have a handsome daughter. If the husband dream it, it implies that his wife will have a son. To dream you see the moon at full, is a good sign to handsome women, of their being beloved by those who view them; but it is bad for such as conceal themselves, as thieves and murderers, for they will certainly be discovered: but it signifies death to those that are sick, and to seafaring men. To dream the moon shines about your bed, implies grace, pardon, and deliverance by some woman. To dream you see the new moon, is a sign of expedition in business. Dreaming you see the moon decrease, betokens the death of some prince or great lord. To dream you see the moon pale, is joyfulness. To dream you see the moon dyed with blood, indicates travel or pilgrimage. Dreaming you see the moon fall from the firmament, is a sign of sickness. To dream you see two moons appear, betokens increase of sorrow. 19, 18.

MOTHER-IN-LAW. Dreaming you see a mother-in-law, dead or alive, is ill; especially if you dream she uses violence or threatening. To dream she uses gentle speech, and gives good enter. tainment, implies vain hope and deceit. 46.

MOUTH. The mouth is the door of all the internal parts of the body, within which they are all enclosed. If, therefore, one dreams that his mouth is wider than ordinary, his family will be enriched, and he will become more opulent than ordinary. If any one dreams that the breath which comes out of his mouth stinks, it implies he shall be despised by all people, and hated by his servants. 27, 6, 3.

MULBERRY-TREE. If one dreams he sees a mulberry-tree, it implies an increase, with abundance of goods and children. 64, 70, 3.

MUSIC. To dream you hear melodious music, which is even ready to ravish your ears, implies the parties dreaming shall hear some very acceptable news, with which they shall be greatly delighted. But if they dream that they hear harsh and ill-tuned music, it means the contrary, and that they shall soon meet with such tidings as they do not wish to hear. 74, 18.

MYRTLE-TREE. In dreams, myrtle-trees signify wanton women; and to dream of them is good for those that would undertake any such business, and to the sick. To others, such dreams signify pain and labor. 3, 11, 33.

NAILS. Dreaming that one's nails are longer than usual, is a sign of profit; and the contrary, loss and discontent. To dream that one's nails are cut off, shows to the party so dreaming that he shall suffer loss and disgrace, and have contention with his friends and relations. 57, 8.

NAVIGATION. To dream of being in a ship or boat, in danger of oversetting and shipwreck, is a sign of danger, unless the party be a prisoner or captive; and in that case it denotes liberty and freedom. He that dreams he falls into the water or the sea, and that he awakes starting, it signifies that he either doth or will enjoy a married woman, and spend his days, substance, and fortune with her. 22.

NETTLES. Dreaming of nettles, and that you sting yourself with them, shows that you will venture hard for what you desire to obtain; and if they are young folks that dream thus, it shows they are in love, and are willing to take a nettle though they are stung thereby. 18.

NIGHT-MARE. To dream of being ridden by the night-mare, is a sign that a woman so dreaming shall be suddenly after married, and that the man shall be ridden and domineered over by a fool. 71.

NIGHT-WALKING. To dream of walking in the night, implies trouble and melancholy. 50.

NOSE. Dreaming one has a fair and great nose, is good to all; for it implies subtlety of sense, providence in affairs, and acquaintance with great persons. But to dream one has no nose, means the contrary; and to a sick man, death; for dead men's heads have no noses. If any one dream his nose is larger than ordinary, he will become rich and powerful, provident and subtle, and be well received among grandees. Dreaming one has two noses, implies discord and quarrels. If one dream his nose is grown so big that it is deformed and hideous to the sight, he will live in prosperity and abundance, but never gain the love of the people. If any one dream his nose is stopped, so that he hath lost his scent, if he be a king, he is in some imminent danger from him that hath the greatest authority about his person. 48.

NUTS. (*See Fruit.*)

OAK. To dream one sees a stately oak, is a sign of long life, riches, and gain to the dreamer. 65.

OIL. Dreaming that you are anointed with oil, is good for women; but for men it is ill, and implies shame. 1, 41.

OLD WOMEN. To dream you are courted by an old woman, and that you marry her, shows you shall have good luck in prosecuting your affairs, but not without some reproaches from the world. 3.

OLIVE-TREES. To dream you see an olive-tree with olives, denotes peace, delight, concord, liberty, dignity, and fruition of your desires. In dreams, the olive-tree means the wife, and therefore it is good to dream that it is flourishing well, bearing fair and ripe fruit in season. To dream you beat the olives down, is good for all but servants. 18.

ORANGES. Dreaming that one sees and eats oranges, implies wounds, grief, vexation, whether they be ripe or not. (*See Fruit.*)

ORGANS. To dream you hear the sound of organs, betokens joy. 55, 3.

OWLS. To dream of owls, old barns, church-yards, &c., betokens much melancholy; as also imprisonment, keeping one's chamber, and sickness: and it denotes the same also to dream of an owlet or bat. 3.

OYSTERS. To dream of opening and eating oysters, shows great hunger, which the party dreaming should suddenly sustain; or else that he should take great pains for his living, as they do that open oysters. 7, 53.

PAPER. To dream you write on, or read in paper, denotes news. To dream you blot or tear your paper, indicates the well ordering of business. 21, 18.

PATHS. Dreaming one walks in large, plain, and easy paths, betokens health to the dreamer; and paths which are narrow, crooked, and rough, signify the contrary. 44.

PEACOCK. To dream you see a peacock, is a sign you will marry a handsome wife, and that you will grow rich, be in great honor, and beloved by the king and grandees. And if the woman has such a dream, it shows that her husband shall be a pretty man, but a sot. 65, 54.

PEACHES. (*See Fruit.*)

PEARS. (*See Fruit.*)

PEAS. Dreaming of peas well boiled, denotes good success and expedition. 6.

PICTURES. To dream one draws pictures, betokens joy without profit. 49.

PIGEONS. To dream you see pigeons, is a good sign; to wit, that you will have content and delight at home, and success in affairs abroad. To dream that you see a white pigeon flying, denotes consolation, devotion, and good success in undertakings, provided they be such as are for the glory of God, and the good of our neighbors. Wild pigeons signify wild and dissolute women, and tame pigeons signify virtuous women. 39.

PISTOLS. (*See Fire-arms.*)

PIT. Dreaming you see a pit full of fair water in a field, where there is none at all, is a good dream; for he who dreams this is a thriving man, and will suddenly be married, if he be not so already, and will have good and obedient children. To dream you see a pit whose water overflows the banks, implies loss of substance, or the death of wife and children; and if the wife have the same dream, it shows her death, or the loss of her substance. To dream you see a friend fall into a pit, shows that such a person is then near his end; and if it be a parent, aunt, or child, that you dream falls, expect to see the death of such relation very suddenly. 54.

PLANT. To dream that any plant cometh out of one's body, is death. To dream of plants quick in growth, as the vine and the peach-tree, implies that the good or evil portended us shall quickly happen; but to dream of trees and plants that are slow in growing, as the oak, olive, cypress, &c., shows that the good or evil that shall happen to us shall be long in coming. 43, 14, 7.

PLAYS. Dreaming you see a comedy, farce, or some other recreation, indicates good success in business. To dream you see a tragedy acted, implies labor, loss of estate, with grief and affliction. To dream one plays, or sees another play upon a lute, violin, or other musical instrument, betokens good news, concord, and a good correspondence between man and wife, master and servant, prince and subject. To dream one plays, or hears, or sees another play upon the virginals, or organs, indicates the death of relations, or funeral obsequies. To dream one plays tunes on small bells, denotes discord and disunion between subjects and servants. To dream you play, or hear playing on wind instruments, as flutes, flageolets, or small bagpipes, or other such instruments, shows trouble, contention, and being overthrown at law. If any one dreams he plays at any of those plays with which company use to divert themselves; as, at questions and commands, cross-purposes, blind-man's buff, hot cockles, barley-break, and such like—it implies prosperity, joy, pleasure, health, and concord among friends and relations. 46.

PLOUGHING. Dreaming of ploughing is good, but if the horses seem to sink into the ground, it portends loss of labor, dearth of corn, and ill harvest weather; but to plough on a hill, and on a sudden to be loosening the team, and setting them up in a stable, doth show a lazy disposition in the ploughman, and also that the horses shall not stand, but fall sick in the stable. 41.

PLUMS. (*See Fruit.*)

POMEGRANATE. If a man dream that he hath gathered the fruit of a pomegranate-tree, he will be enriched by some wealthy person. But if the pomegranate be not ripe, it denotes sickness, and affliction by some person wickedly disposed. (*See Fruit.*)

POTHERBS. To dream of potherbs, especially such as have a strong smell, portends a discovery of hidden secrets and domestic jars. 30.

PRAYERS. Dreaming you put up prayers and supplications to God, implies happiness. The prayers of beggars, and of the poor and miserable, signify care and anger to those who dream thereof; for no one requesteth of another without affliction; none that are afflicted have reason and consideration, by reason whereof they are importunate, and cause trouble and hindrance. 1.

PREDECESSORS. To dream of predecessors, as grandfathers and other ancestors, implies care. 9.

PURSE. To dream that one hath lost his purse, is good and auspicious, if it be old and empty: for then thereby it is a sign that the party dreaming shall either have a new one, or one that is full; but if he dreamed he found it again, he must even be content with the old, for he is like to have no other. 78.

QUAGMIRE. Dreaming one has fallen into a quagmire, shows the party so dreaming shall meet with such obstructions in his affairs, as shall be very difficult to overcome. 14.

QUARRELS. If a man dream of quarrels and fighting, he shall hear of some unlooked for news of women, or embrace some joy he thought not of. 2, 12, 24.

QUESTIONS AND COMMANDS. Dreaming one is at play at questions and commands, with many others, implies prosperity, joy, pleasure, health, and concord among friends and relations. 23.

QUICKSILVER. (*See Metals.*)

QUINCE. To dream one sees quinces, shows that they shall meet with some changes in their affairs, which shall be for the better. 49, 6.

RADISHES. To dream that one eats or smells of radishes, signifies a discovery of hidden secrets, and domestic jars. 38, 13.

RAINBOW. To dream you see a rainbow in the sky, betokens the changing of your present estate and manner of life. 45.

RASPBERRIES. (*See Fruit.*)

READING. To dream you are reading romances, comedies,

or other diverting books, signifies joy and comfort. To dream you read serious books, and of some divine science, denotes wisdom. 65, 2.

RELATIONS DECEASED. To dream one sees and discourses with father, mother, wife, brother, sister, or some other of his relations and friends, though they are dead, is an advertisement for the party to mind his affairs, and to behave himself properly in the world. 70.

RICE. To dream of eating rice, denotes abundance of obstruction. 12, 2, 24.

RIDE. To dream you ride with a company of men, is very lucky and profitable; but with women, it signifies misfortune and deceit. 6, 12, 72.

RINGS. To dream of rings, betokeneth weddings, because they are then required. 4, 20.

RIVER. To dream you see a river water clear and calm, presages good to all persons. To dream of swimming in a great river, signifies future peril and danger. 34, 20.

ROOTS. All roots which have a strong smell in eating, signify the revealing of secrets and anger. Roots which are pared or scraped before they are eaten, signify hurt, by reason of the superfluity which is cast away. 35.

ROSES. To dream of seeing and smelling roses in the season of the year, is a good sign for all persons. If the dream be when roses are out of season, it signifies the contrary. Also, to dream of gathering roses, denotes the want of fruition, and folly of love. But to dream you see red roses, is a sign of joy, recreation, pleasure, and delight. 47, 9.

SADDLE. To dream you were riding a horse without a saddle, signifies poverty, disgrace, and shame to the dreamer. 2.

SEA. To dream of walking upon the sea, is good to him who would travel, as also to a servant, and to him who would take a wife; for the one shall enjoy his wife, and the other shall have his master at his own pleasure. 6.

SERPENTS. To dream you see a serpent turning and winding himself, signifies danger and imprisonment; it denotes, also, sickness and hatred. To dream you see many serpents, signifies you will be deceived by your wife. 27.

SHIPWRECK. To dream you see a shipwreck, is most dangerous to all, except those who are detained by force; for to them it signifieth releasing and liberty. 12.

SHOWER. If one dream he sees a soft shower, without storm, tempest, or wind, it signifies gain. 39.

SILVER. (See Metals.)

SINGING. If any one dreams he sings, it signifies he will be affected, and weep. To dream you hear singing, or playing in concert upon instruments, signifies consolation in adversity, and recovery of health to those that are sick. 34, 18.

STEEL. (*See Metals.*)

STRAWBERRIES. (*See Fruit.*)

TAPESTRY. To dream that one makes tapestry, signifies joy. To dream you see tapestry, denotes treachery, deceit, and cozenage. 75.

TAVERN. To dream you are in a tavern, and feasting with your companions, signifies joy and comfort. 46, 33.

TEMPEST. To dream of great and long continuing tempests, signifies affliction, troubles, danger, losses, and peril; to the poorer sort they denote repose. 57, 8.

TIN. (*See Metals.*)

TREASURE. To dream you find treasure hid in the earth, is evil, whether it be little or great; for they open the earth for the dead, as well as for treasure. (*See Metals.*)

VINEGAR. To dream that you drink vinegar, betokens sickness. 29, 6, 76.

VIRGIN. To dream you discourse with the Virgin Mary, signifies joy and consolation; but a virgin dreaming she has lost her virtue, denotes she will give herself up to the first she likes. 54, 3.

VOMIT. To dream of vomiting, whether of blood, meat, or phlegm, signifies to the poor profit; to the rich hurt; for the first can lose nothing till they have it, but the others, who have goods already, shall come to lose them. 14, 65.

WALNUTS. To dream that one sees and eats walnuts, or hazel-nuts, signifies difficulty and trouble. 48, 6.

WATCH. To dream that in the night one sitteth up, and watcheth in the chamber, signifies, to the rich, great affairs; to the poor, and those that would use any subtleties or deceits, it is good; for the first shall not be without work and gain, and the others, undergoing their attempts with great subtlety, shall come to the height of their enterprise. 42, 11.

WEDDINGS. For a man that is sick, to dream that he is wedded to a maid, shows that he shall die quickly. If one dreams he is wedded to a deformed woman, it signifies discontent; if to a handsome woman, it denotes joy and profit. 42, 78, 2.

WIFE. If a man dreams he sees his wife married to another, it betokens a change of affairs, or else of separation. If a man's wife dream she is married to any other than her own husband, she shall be separated from him, or see him dead. 22.

YACHT. To dream you are sailing a yacht or boat in rough or stormy weather, indicates that you will be very successful in business, and happy in love or domestic matters, providing the water looks clear and green. If the water looks black or muddy, it is a sign you will soon have some sort of trouble. If the water is smooth and clear, it portends that a rich relative will die and leave you a fortune. 21, 1.

ZINC. (*See Metals.*)

PALMISTRY;

OR, TELLING FORTUNES BY THE LINES OF THE HAND.

FOR this purpose, the left hand is always the one chosen, it being supposed that the heart and brain have more influence over it than its fellow. The art of palmistry is no guess-work, as many persons suppose—but is founded upon, and determined by simple rules and long observation.

The practical part of palmistry, is that which gathereth probable predictions from lines, the places of the planets in the hand, and from the notes and characters everywhere pointed and marked out in the hands and fingers. Our readers will therefore be careful to let the following rules be duly observed:—

In the first place each finger has its name.

(1)	Forefinger:	Jupiter	♃
(2)	Middle finger:	Saturn	♄
(3)	Ring finger:	The Sun	☉
(4)	Little finger:	Mercury	☿
(5)	Thumb:	Venus	♀

Each hand has five main lines.

(1)	The Life line:	Vitalis.
(2)	The Natural line.	Naturalis.
(3)	The Table line:	Mensalis.
(4)	The Liver line:	Hepatica.
(5)	The Wrist line:	Rascetta.

(See Engraving.)

1. VITALIS; OR, THE LINE OF LIFE.

The principal line in the hand is called *Vitalis*, or the line of Life.

This being broad, of a lively color, and decently drawn in its bounds, without intersections and points, shows the party long lived, and subject but to few diseases.

If slender, short, and dissected with obverse little lines; and deformed either by a pale or black color, it presageth weakness of the body, sickness, and a short life.

If the line of Life is anywhere broken, it threatens extreme danger of life in that part of the age which the break in the line shows. The line of

Life begins between ♃ and ♀ (the thumb and forefinger), and the length of life is in proportion to the length of the line of Life. If you wish to find out the dangerous years of your age, you must divide the line into seventy parts, and commence to count the number of divisions, beginning from Rascetta, or Wrist line, and the number falling where the line is broken, shows your unlucky or unhealthy year.

In most cases, one or more lines run from the Natural line to the line of Life. This indicates the partner of one's life. The point where the junction takes place denotes the point of time of the marriage. If this occurs near the commencement of the line, of course the marriage will take place early in life. If two lines unite with the line of Life, it indicates two husbands (or wives). If no line joins it, the person will remain unmarried.

2. NATURALIS; OR, NATURAL LINE.

The next line in importance is Naturalis, or the Natural line. This line takes its beginning at ♃, and runs to ☿. If this line is straight and continued, and not dissected by lines, it denotes a strong constitution, excellent digestive organs, and an amiable disposition. Large crosses in this line, signify imprudence, loss of property, and a fiery temper.

3. MENSALIS; OR, THE TABLE LINE.

Mensalis, or the Table line, commonly known as the line of Fortune, begins under ☿ and ends under ♃. If this line is broad and fair, without being broken, it is a sign that, with care and industry, the person will lead a happy life; but if broken, it shows that great prudence is needed to avert threatened misfortune. If well defined, this line indicates an amorous temperament, and signifies good fortune in love and wedlock.

Sometimes little lines sprout from this one and run between the fingers, or opposite the base of the fingers. If one of these lines terminates at the base of ♄, it denotes wealth and honors; if at ☉, it foretells success in love; if between ♄ and ☉, it is a sign of sorrow and disappointment; if between ♃ and ♄, you will some day lose a large sum of money, either by being cheated, or making a bad bargain.

From the ring finger (Solis ☉) there commonly runs one or more lines into the Table line. These denote the various inclinations of the heart. If but a single line is actually visible, and if this is deep and long, the person loves or will love faithfully and warmly. If a number of smaller lines are found in its place, the person is inconstancy itself, a butterfly roving from flower to flower. Add up all these little lines, and the sum will give you the number of times the person will fall in love.

4. HEPATICA; OR, THE LIVER LINE.

This line runs from the outside of the hand under ☿ to the base of ♃. If it is straight and strongly defined, it signifies a robust constitution, a merry disposition, and great intelligence. If it is short and broken, it foretells sickness and death. If it throws out branches near its commencement, it portends a mischievous inclination to play pranks; it also shows wit, acuteness, great determination, and presence of mind.

5. RASCETTA; OR, THE WRIST LINE.

When this line is perfect and unbroken, it signifies good fortune in all matters of importance. It portends health, strength, success in love and money matters, and a happy and long life. If the Rascetta line is broken and imperfect, it portends a long life, and final success, after enduring many hardships and trials.

OBSERVATIONS ON THE FINGERS.

The structure of the hand itself is most admirable in respect to the proportion it beareth to the face, and certain parts thereof, which is this:—

1. The whole hand is of equal length with the face.

2. The greater joint of the forefinger equals the height of the forehead.

3. The other two (to the extremity of the nail) is just the length of the nose, viz., from the intercelia, or place between the eyebrows, to the tip of the nostrils.

4. The first and greater joint of the middle finger, is just as long as it is between the bottom of the chin and the top of the under lip.

5. But the third joint of the same finger is of equal length, with the distance that is between the mouth and the lower part of the nostrils.

6. The largest joint of the thumb gives the width of the mouth.

7. The distance between the bottom of the chin and the top of the lower lip, the same.

8. The lesser joint of the thumb is equal to the distance between the top of the under lip and the lower part of the nostrils. The nails obtain just the half of their respective uppermost joints, which they call omychios.

HOW TO TELL A PERSON'S CHARACTER

BY MEANS OF CABALISTIC CALCULATIONS.

THIS is said to have been the invention of the sage Pythagoras, whose doctrine was that every thing in the universe was represented and governed by certain figures or numbers, to which he ascribed mysterious properties and virtues. According to him, every thing, from the Supreme Being himself, down to the minutest atom, was distinguished by its own proper number; and his belief was shared by numberless other philosophers. Without entering into any detail of this system, we will proceed to describe how these calculations are made. An alphabetical table must be first prepared, with its corresponding numbers, thus:—

A	B	C	D	E	F	G	H	I
1	2	3	4	5	6	7	8	9
K	L	M	N	O	P	Q	R	S
10	20	30	40	50	60	70	80	90
T	U	X	Y	Z	J	V	Hi	Hu
100	200	300	400	500	600	700	800	900

This is accompanied by a list of numbers, with their various interpretations and significations, as follows:—

1. Passion, ambition, design.
2. Destruction, death, catastrophe.
3. Religion, destiny, the soul, charms.
4. Solidity, wisdom, power.
5. The stars, happiness, graces, marriage.
6. Perfection, labor.
7. Course of life, repose, liberty, perfect happiness.
8. Justice, preservation.
9. Imperfection, diminution, grief, pain, expectation
10. Success, reason, future happiness.
11. Faults, punishment, discord, prevarication.
12. Good omen, a town, or city.
13. Impiety.
14. Sacrifice, purification.
15. Piety, self-culture.
16. Love, happiness, voluptuousness.
17. Misfortune, forgetfulness.
18. Hardening of the heart, misfortune.
19. Folly.
20. Austerity, sadness.
21. Mystery, wisdom, the creation.
22. A scourge, the divine vengeance.

23. Ignorance of the doctrines of Christianity.
24. A journey.
25. Intelligence, a birth.
26. Useful works.
27. Firmness, courage.
28. Love tokens.
29. Letters.
30. Fame, a wedding.
31. Love of glory, virtue.
32. Marriage.
33. Purity.
34. Suffering trouble of mind.
35. Health, harmony.
36. Genius, vast conception.
37. Domestic virtues, conjugal love.
38. Imperfection, avarice, envy.
39. Praise.
40. Fetes, wedding.
41. Ignominy.
42. A short and unhappy life, the tomb.
43. Religious ceremonies, a priest.
44. Power, pomp, monarchy.
45. Population.
46. Fertility.
47. Long and happy life.
48. Tribunal, judgment, judge.
49. Love of money.
50. Pardon, liberty.
60. Widowhood.
70. Initiated, science, the graces.
75. The world.
77. Pardon, repentance.
80. A cure.
81. An adept.
90. Blindness, error, affliction.
100. Divine favor.
120. Patriotism, praises.
200. Irresolution.
215. Calamity.
300. Safety, belief, faith, philosophy.
318. Divine messenger.
350. Hope, justice.
360. Home, society.
365. Astronomy.
400. Long and wearisome voyage.
490. Priests, theology.
500. Holiness.
600. Perfection.

666. A malicious person, machinations, plots, enemies.
700. Strength.
800. Empire.
900. War, combats, struggles.
1000. Mercy.
1095. Taciturnity.
1260. Torments.
1390. Persecution.

Now write down the name of the person whose character you wish to learn, and beneath each letter composing it place the corresponding number. (Should the letter W be one of them, it must be represented by two Vs, which will give the number 1,400.) Add them all together, and by comparing the product with the table of significations, you will discover what you wish to know. When the product exceeds the highest number given in the table, the first number is cut off, and the remainder alone used. We give an example, supposing the name to be Jean Jacques Rousseau:—

J	600	J	600	R	80
E	5	A	1	O	50
A	1	C	3	U	200
N	40	Q	70	S	90
	——	U	200	S	90
	646	E	5	E	5
	——	S	90	A	1
			——	U	200
			969		——
			——		716

646 Jean.
969 Jacques.
716 Rousseau.

2331 Total.

Of this total of 2,331, we cut off the 2,000, leaving 331, which, on reference to the table of significations, reads as follows:—Belief, faith, and philosophy, for 300; love of glory, virtue, for 31; giving no bad sketch of his character. It may be as well to observe that, when the total consists of a number not precisely marked on

the table, the answer may be obtained by dividing it into hun'
dreds, tens, and units; thus, supposing the number obtained was
179, it could be divided into 100, 70, and 9. Care must be taken
to add up the lines of figures correctly, as the slightest mistake
will of course entirely change the whole meaning.

FORTUNE TELLING

BY THE GROUNDS IN A TEA OR COFFEE CUP.

POUR the grounds of tea or coffee into a white cup; shake them
well about, so as to spread them over the surface; reverse the
cup to drain away the superfluous contents, and then exercise
your fertile fancy in discovering what the figures thus formed
represent. Long, wavy lines denote vexations and losses—their
importance depending on the number of lines. Straight ones,
on the contrary, foretell peace, tranquillity, and long life. Human
figures are usually good omens, announcing love affairs, and marriage. If circular figures predominate, the person for whom the
experiment is made, may expect to receive money. If these cir-
cles are connected by straight, unbroken lines, there will be delay,
but ultimately all will be satisfactory, Squares, foretell peace and
happiness; oblong figures, family discord; whilst curved, twisted,
or angular ones, are certain signs of vexations and annoyances,
their probable duration being determined by the number of figures
A crown, signifies honor; a cross, news of death; a ring, marriage—if a letter can be discovered near it, that will be the initial
of the name of the future spouse. If the ring is in the clear part
of the cup, it foretells a happy union; if clouds are about it, the
contrary; but if it should chance to be quite at the bottom, then
the marriage will never take place. A leaf of clover, or trefoil, is
a good sign, denoting, if at the top of the cup, speedy good fortune, which will be more or less distant in case it appears at, or
near the bottom. The anchor, if at the bottom of the cup, denotes
success in business; at the top, and in the clear part, love and
fidelity; but in thick, or cloudy parts, inconstancy. The serpent
is always the sign of an enemy, and if in the cloudy part, gives
warning that great prudence will be necessary to ward off misfortune. The coffin, portends news of a death, or long illness. The
dog, at the top of the cup, denotes true and faithful friends; in
the middle, that they are not to be trusted; but at the bottom,
that they are secret enemies. The lily, at the top of the cup, foretells a happy marriage; at the bottom, anger. A letter, signifies
news; if in the clear, very welcome ones; surrounded by dots,
a remittance of money; but if hemmed in by clouds, bad tidings,
and losses. A heart near it, denotes a love letter. A single tree

portends restoration to health; a group of trees in the clear, misfortunes, which may be avoided; several trees, wide apart, promise that your wishes will be accomplished; if encompassed by dashes, it is a token that your fortune is in its blossom, and only requires care to bring to maturity; if surrounded by dots, riches. Mountains signify either friends or enemies, according to their situation. The sun, moon, and stars, denote happiness, success. The clouds, happiness or misfortune, according as they are bright or dark. Birds are good omens, but quadrupeds—with the exception of the dog—foretell trouble and difficulties. Fish, imply good news from across the water. A triangle, portends an unexpected legacy; a single straight line, a journey. The figure of a man, indicates a speedy visitor; if the arm is outstretched, a present; when the figure is very distinct, it shows that the person expected will be of dark complexion, and *vice versâ*. A crown, near a cross, indicates a large fortune, resulting from a death. Flowers, are signs of joy, happiness, and peaceful life. A heart, surrounded by dots, signifies joy, occasioned by the receipt of money; with a ring near it, approaching marriage.

HOW TO READ YOUR FORTUNE BY THE WHITE OF AN EGG.

BREAK a new-laid egg, and, carefully separating the yolk from the white, drop the latter into a large tumbler half full of water; place this, uncovered, in some dry place, and let it remain untouched for four-and-twenty hours, by which time the white of the egg will have formed itself into various figures—rounds, squares, ovals, animals, trees, crosses, &c.—which are to be interpreted in the same manner as those formed by the coffee grounds. Of course, the more whites there are in the glass, the more figures there will be.

This is a very pretty experiment, and much practised by the young Scotch maidens, who, however, believe it to have more efficacy when tried on either Midsummer Eve or Hallowe'en (31st October).

HOW TO TELL FORTUNES

BY THE MOLES ON A PERSON'S BODY.

A MOLE that stands on the right side of the forehead, or right temple, signifies that the person will arrive to sudden wealth and honor.

2. A mole on the right eyebrow, announces speedy marriage, the husband to possess many good qualities and a large fortune.

3. A mole on the left of either of those three places, portends unexpected disappointment in your most sanguine wishes.

4. A mole on the outside of either eye, denotes the person to be of a steady, sober, and sedate disposition.

5. A mole on either cheek, signifies that the person never shall rise above mediocrity in point of fortune.

6. A mole on the nose, shows that the person will have good success in his or her undertakings.

7. A mole on the lip, either upper or lower, proves the person to be fond of delicate things, and much given to the pleasures o' love, in which he or she will most commonly be successful.

8. A mole on the chin, indicates that the person will be attended with great prosperity, and be highly esteemed.

9. A mole on the side of the neck, shows that the person will narrowly escape suffocation; but will afterward rise to great consideration by an unexpected legacy or inheritance.

10. A mole on the throat, denotes that the person shall become rich by marriage.

11. A mole on the right breast, declares the person to be exposed to a sudden reverse from comfort to distress, by unavoidable accidents. Most of his children will be girls.

12. A mole on the left breast, signifies success in undertakings, and an amorous disposition. Most of his children will be boys.

13. A mole on the bosom, portends mediocrity of health and fortune.

14. A mole under the left breast, over the heart, foreshows that a man will be of a warm disposition, unsettled in mind, fond of rambling, and light in his conduct. In a lady it shows sincerity in love, and easy travail in child-birth.

15. A mole on the right side over any part of the ribs, denotes the person to be pusillanimous, and slow in understanding any thing that may be attended with difficulties.

16. A mole on the belly, shows the person to be addicted to sloth and gluttony, and not very choice in point of dress.

17. A mole on either hip, shows that the person will have many children, and that they will be healthy and possess much patience.

18. A mole on the right thigh, is an indication of riches, and much happiness in the married state.

19. A mole on the left thigh, denotes poverty and want of friends through the enmity and injustice of others.

20. A mole on the right knee, shows the person will be fortunate in the choice of a partner for life, and meet with few disappointments in the world.

21. A mole on the left knee, portends that the person will be rash, inconsiderate, and hasty, but modest when in cool blood.

22. A mole on either leg, shows that the person is indolent, thoughtless, and indifferent as to whatever may happen.

23. A mole on either ankle, denotes a man to be inclined to

effeminacy and elegance of dress; a lady to be courageous, active and industrious, with a trifle of the termagant.

24. A mole on either foot, forebodes sudden illness or unexpected misfortune.

25. A mole on the right shoulder, indicates prudence, discretion, secrecy, and wisdom.

26. A mole on the left shoulder, declares a testy, contentious, and ungovernable spirit.

27. A mole on the right arm, denotes vigor and an undaunted courage.

28. A mole on the left arm, declares resolution and victory in battle.

29. A mole near either elbow, denotes restlessness, a roving and unsteady temper, also a discontentedness with those which they are obliged to live constantly with.

30. A mole between the elbow and the wrist, promises the person prosperity, but not until he has undergone many hardships.

31. A mole on the wrist, or between it, and the ends of the fingers, shows industry, parsimony, and conjugal affection.

32. A mole on any part, from the shoulders to the loins, is indicative of imperceptible decline and gradual decay, whether of health or wealth.

THE ART OF DISCOVERING TRUTH FROM FALSEHOOD.

IF you suspect your servant, or any other person of telling a lie or false story, that may be to your prejudice, or otherwise, be not so rash as to charge them with it directly, but try the following rule of art, to inform you for a certainty of that which you can at present only surmise or suspect, without any real ground:

Write the name of the party, and the name of the day the discourse took place, which you cannot believe, and then mind the following alphabet and figures:

A 10	B 2	C 20	D 4	E 14	F 6	G 16	H 7
I 20	K 11	L 1	M 12	N 4	O 14	P 6	Q 18
R 18	S 18	T 10	V 2	X 2	Y 4	Z 14	

Take the letters and figures belonging to them, that will make the name of the party suspected, as well as those that form the name of the day, to which add 26, then divide the whole; should the remainder be odd, you may rest assured the party told you an untruth, which you may charge them with, and either by open confession, blushes, or some other sign, you may easily discover the deception. But, on the contrary, if it be even, you may rely on the truth of what has been told you.

LIST OF UNLUCKY DAYS,

WHICH, TO MALES BORN ON THEM WILL, AS A GENE-RAL THING, PROVE UNFORTUNATE.

January 3, 4.
February 6, 7, 12, 13, 19, 20.
March 5, 6, 12, 13.
May 12, 13, 20, 21, 26, 27.
June 1, 2, 9, 10, 16, 17, 22, 23, 24.
July 3, 4, 10, 11, 16, 17, 18.
October 3, 4, 9, 10, 11, 16, 17, 31.
November 1, 3.

Almost all persons (being of the male sex) that are born on the days included in the foregoing table, will, in a greater or less degree suffer, not only by pecuniary embarrassment and losses of property, but will also experience great distress and anxiety of mind, much dissatisfaction, dissension, and unhappiness in their family affairs, much disaffection to each other among the married ones (indeed few of them can *ever* be happy in the married state), trouble about their children, daughters forming unfortunate attachments, and a variety of untoward events of other descriptions which our limits do not allow us to particularize. The influence of these days are of a quality and tendency calculated to excite in the minds of persons born on them, an extraordinary itch for speculation, to make changes in their affairs, commence new undertakings of various kinds, but all of them will tend nearly to one point—loss of property and pecuniary embarrassments. Such persons who embark their capital on credit in new concerns or engagements, will be likely to receive checks or interruptions to the progress of their schemes or undertakings. Those who enter into engagements intended to be permanent, whether purchases, leases, partnerships, or in short any other speculation of a description which cannot readily be transferred, or got rid of, will dearly *repent their bargains.*

They will find their affairs from time to time much interrupted and agitated, and experience many disappointments in money matters, trouble through bills, and have need of all their activity and address to prop their declining credit; indeed almost all engagements and affairs that are entered upon by persons born on any of these days will receive some sort of check or obstruction. The greater number of those persons born on these days will be subject to weakness or sprains in the knees and ancles, also diseases and hurts in the legs.

LIST OF UNLUCKY DAYS,

WHICH, TO FEMALES BORN ON THEM, WILL GENERALLY PROVE UNFORTUNATE.

January 5, 6, 13, 14, 20, and 21.
February 2, 3, 9, 10, 16, 17, 22, and 23.
March 1, 2, 8, 9, 16, 17, 28, and 29.
April 24 and 25,
May 1, 2, 9, 17, 22, 29, and 30.
June 5, 6, 12, 13, 18, and 19
July 3 and 4.
September 9 and 16.
October 20 and 27.
November 9, 10, 21, 29, and 30
December 6, 14, and 21.

We particularly advise all females born on these days to be extremely cautious of placing their affections too hastily, as they will be subject to *disappointments* and *vexations* in that respect; it will be better for them (in those matters) to be guided by the advice of their friends, rather than by their own feelings, they will be less fortunate in placing their affections, than in any other action of their lives, as many of these marriages will terminate in separations, divorces, &c. Their courtships will end in elopements, seductions, and other ways not necessary of explanation. Our readers must be well aware that affairs of importance begun at inauspicious times, by those who have been born at those periods when the stars shed their malign influence, can seldom, if ever, lead to much good: it is, therefore, that we endeavor to lay before them a correct statement drawn from accurate astrological information, in order that by strict attention and care, they may avoid falling into those perplexing labyrinths from which nothing but that care and attention can save them. The list of days we have above given, will be productive of hasty and clandestine marriages—marriages under untoward circumstances, perplexing attachments, and, as a natural consequence, the displeasure of friends, together with family broils, dissensions, and divisions. We now present our readers with a

LIST OF DAYS

USUALLY CONSIDERED FORTUNATE,

*With respect to Courtship, Marriage, and Love affairs in general.—
Females that were born on the following days may expect Courtships and prospects of Marriage, and which will have a happy
termination.*

January 1, 2, 15, 26, 27, 28.
February 11, 21, 25, 26.
March 10, 24.
April 6, 15, 16, 20, 28.
May 3, 13, 18, 31.
June 10, 11, 15, 22, 25.
July 9, 14, 15, 28.
August 6, 7, 10, 11, 16, 20, 25.
September 4, 8, 9, 17, 18, 23.
October 3, 7, 16, 21, 22.
November 5, 14, 20.
December 14, 15, 19, 20, 22, 23, 25.

Although the greater number, or indeed nearly all the ladies
that are born on the days stated in the preceding list, will be
likely to meet with a *prospect* of marriage, or become engaged in
some love affair of *more* than ordinary importance, yet it must not
be expected that the *result* will be the same with all of them;
with some they will *terminate* in *marriage*—with others in disappointment—and some of them will be in danger of forming *attachments* that may prove of a somewhat *troublesome* description.
We shall, therefore, in order to enable our readers to distinguish
them, give a comprehensive and useful list, showing which of
them will be most likely to marry.

Those born within the limits of the succeeding List of Hours,
on any of the preceding days, will be the most likely to *marry*—or
will, at least, have *Courtships* that will be likely to have a happy
termination.

LIST OF FORTUNATE HOURS.

January 2d. From 30 minutes past 10 till 15 minutes past 1
in the morning; and from 15 minutes before 9 till 15 minutes
before 11 at night.

15th. From 30 minutes past 9 till 15 minutes past 10 in the
morning; and from 30 minutes past 7 till 15 minutes past 11
at night.

26th. From 30 minutes past 8 till 15 minutes past 9 in the
morning; and from 7 till 15 minutes past 10 at night.

February 11th and 12th.   From 30 minutes past 7 till 15 minutes past 8 in the morning; and from 15 minutes past 6 till 15 minutes before 9 at night.

   21st.   From 7 till 15 minutes before 8 in the morning; and from 15 minutes past 5 till 15 minutes before 8 at night.

   25th and 26th.   From 15 minutes before 7 till 30 minutes past 7 in the morning; and from 15 minutes before 5 till 30 minutes past 7 in the evening.

March 10th.   From 5 till 15 minutes before 6 in the morning; and from 4 in the afternoon till 15 minutes before 7 in the evening.

April 6th.   From 15 minutes past 4 till 5 in the morning; and from 30 minutes past 2 till 15 minutes past 5 in the afternoon.

   20th.   From 30 minutes past 3 till 15 minutes past 4 in the morning; and from 30 minutes past 1 till 15 minutes past 4 in the afternoon.

May 3d.   From 15 minutes before 3 till 30 minutes past 3 in the morning; and from 15 minutes before 1 till 30 minutes past 3 in the afternoon.

   13th.   From 2 till 15 minutes before 3 in the morning; and from 12 at noon till 15 minutes before 3 in the afternoon.

   18th.   From 15 minutes before 1 till 30 minutes past 2 in the morning; and from 15 minutes before 12 at noon till 30 minutes past 2 in the afternoon.

   31st.   From 15 minutes before 1 till 30 minutes past 1 in the morning; and from 15 minutes past 10 in the morning till 15 minutes before 1 in the afternoon.

June 10th and 11th.   From 15 minutes past 10 till 1 in the afternoon; and from 12 at night till 1 in the morning.

   15th.   From 10 in the morning till 2 in the afternoon; and from 15 minutes before 12 at night till 15 minutes before 1 in the morning.

   25th.   From 15 minutes past 9 in the morning till 12 at noon; and from 11 to 12 at night.

   29th.   From 9 in the morning till 15 minutes before 12 at noon; and from 15 minutes before 11 till 15 minutes before 12 at night.

July 9th.   From 15 minutes past 8 till 11 in the morning; and from 10 till 11 at night.

   14th and 15th.   From 8 till 11 in the morning; and from 10 till 11 at night.

   28th.   From 7 till 10 in the morning; and from 9 till 10 at night.

August 6th and 7th.   From 30 minutes past 6 till 15 minutes past 9 in the morning; and from 15 minutes past 8 till 15 minutes past 9 at night.

   10th and 11th.   From 15 minutes past 6 till 9 in the morning; and from 8 till 9 in the evening.

   19th and 20th.   From 30 minutes past 5 till 30 minutes past 8 in the morning; and from 30 minutes past 7 till 30 minutes past 8 in the evening.

25th. From 15 minutes past 5 till 8 in the morning; and from 7 till 8 in the evening.

September 4th. From 15 minutes before 5 till 30 minutes past 7 in the morning; and from 30 minutes past 6 till 30 minutes past 7 in the evening.

8th and 9th. From 30 minutes past 4 till 15 minutes past 7 in the morning; and from 15 minutes past 6 till 15 minutes past 7 in the evening.

17th and 18th. From 5 till 15 minutes after 5 in the morning; and from 15 minutes before 6 till 15 minutes before 7 in the evening.

23d. From 30 minutes past 3 till 30 minutes past 5 in the morning; and from 30 minutes past 5 till 30 minutes past 6 in the evening.

October 3d. From 3 till 15 minutes before 6 in the morning; and from 15 minutes past 4 till 15 minutes past 5 in the afternoon.

7th. From 15 minutes before 3 till 30 minutes past 5 in the morning; and from 30 minutes past 4 till 30 minutes past 5 in the afternoon.

16th. From 2 till 5 in the morning; and from 4 till 5 in the afternoon.

21st and 22d. From 15 minutes before 2 till 30 minutes past 4 in the morning; and from 30 minutes past 3 till 15 minutes past 4 in the afternoon.

November 5th. From 1 till 15 minutes before 4 in the morning; and from 15 minutes before 3 till 15 minutes before 4 in the afternoon.

14th. From 15 minutes past 12 till 3 in the morning; and from 2 till 3 in the afternoon.

20th. From 15 minutes before 12 till 15 minutes past 2 in the morning; and from 15 minutes past 1 till 2 in the afternoon.

December 14th and 15th. From 10 till 30 minutes past 12 in the morning; and from 12 at noon till 15 minutes before 1 in the afternoon.

18th and 19th. From 15 minutes before 10 at night till 15 minutes past 5 in the morning; and from 30 minutes past 11 till 15 minutes past 12 at night.

January 3d. From 30 minutes past 10 till 15 minutes past 11 in the morning; and from 15 minutes before 9 till 15 minutes past 11 at night.

12th and 13th. From 15 minutes past 9 till 10 in the morning; and from 15 minutes before 8 till 30 minutes past 10 at night.

18th. From 9 till 15 minutes before 10 in the morning; and from 15 minutes past 7 till 10 at night.

27th. From 9 till 15 minutes before 10 in the morning; and from 7 till 15 minutes before 10 at night.

February 1st. From 8 till 30 minutes past 8 in the morning; and from 6 till 30 minutes past 8 in the evening.

11th and 12th. From 15 minutes before 8 till 30 minutes past 8 in the morning; and from 15 minutes before 6 till 30 minutes past 8 in the evening.

17th. From 7 till 15 minutes before 8 in the morning; and from 15 minutes past 5 till 8 in the evening.

March 1st. From 30 minutes past 6 till 15 minutes past 7 in the morning; and from 30 minutes past 4 till 15 minutes past 7 in the evening.

16th and 17th. From 30 minutes past 5 till 15 minutes past 6 in the morning; and from 15 minutes before 4 till 30 minutes past 6 in the evening.

19th, 20th, 21st, 22d, 23d, 24th, and 25th. From 30 minutes past 5 till 30 minutes past 6 in the morning; and from 30 minutes past 3 till 15 minutes past 6 in the evening.

26th, 27th, 28th, 29th, and 30th. From 15 minutes past 5 till 15 minutes before 6 in the morning; and from 15 minutes past 3 till 6 in the evening.

April 3d, 4th, 5th, 6th, 7th, 8th, and 9th. From 30 minutes past 4 till 30 minutes past 5 in the morning; and from 30 minutes past 2 till 5 in the afternoon.

10th, 11th, 12th, 13th, and 14th. From 15 minutes before 4 till 15 minutes before 5 in the morning; and from 2 till 30 minutes past 4 in the afternoon.

19th, 20th, 21st, 22d, and 23d. From 30 minutes past 4 in the morning; and from 15 minutes before 2 till 30 minutes past 4 in the afternoon.

April 25th, 26th, 27th and 28th. From 3 till 4 in the morning; and from 15 minutes past 1 till 15 minutes before 4 in the afternoon.

May 3d, 4th, 5th, 6th, 7th, and 8th. From 15 minutes past 2 till 15 minutes past 3 in the morning; and from 30 minutes past 12 at noon till 15 minutes past 3 in the afternoon.

9th, 10th, 11th, 12th, and 13th. From 2 till 3 in the morning; and from 15 minutes past 12 at noon till 3 in the afternoon.

16th, 17th, 18th, 19th, 20th, 21st, and 22d. From 15 minutes before 2 till 15 minutes before 3 in the morning; and from 12 at noon till 15 minutes before 3 in the afternoon.

23d, 24th, 25th, 26th, and 27th. From 15 minutes past 1 till 15 minutes past 2 in the morning; and from 30 minutes past 11 in the forenoon till 15 minutes past 2 in the afternoon.

June 1st, 2d, 3d, 4th, 5th, and 6th. From 15 minutes past 10 in the morning till 1 in the afternoon; and from 15 minutes past 12 at night till 15 minutes past 1 the next morning.

11th. From 15 minutes past 10 in the morning, till 15 minutes before 1 in the afternoon; and from 12 at night till 1 the next morning.

20th. From 30 minutes past 9 in the morning till 12 at noon; and from 11 to 12 at night.

25th. From 15 minutes past 9 in the morning till 15 minutes past 12 at noon; and from 11 till 12 at night.

July 5th. From 15 minutes before 8 till 15 minutes past 10 in the morning; and from 15 minutes before 10 till 15 minutes ·before 11 at night.

6th. From 15 minutes past 8 till 11 in the morning; and from 15 minutes past 10 till 11 at night.

19th. From 30 minutes past 7 till 10 in the morning; and from 15 minutes past 9 till 15 minutes past 10 at night.

24th. From 7 till 15 minutes before 10 in the morning; and from 9 till 10 at night.

August 2d and 3d. From 30 minutes past 6 till 15 minutes before 9 in the morning; and from 30 minutes past 8 till 30 minutes past 9 at night.

6th. From 15 minutes before 6 till 9 in the morning; and from 30 minutes past 7 till 30 minutes past 8 at night.

22d. From 15 minutes past 5 till 8 in the morning; and from 15 minutes past 7 till 15 minutes past 8 at night.

September 1st. From 4 till 15 minutes before 7 in the morning; and from 6 till 7 in the evening.

5th. From 30 minutes past 4 till 15 minutes before 7 in the morning; and from 30 minutes past 6 till 30 minutes past 7 in the evening.

14th. From 15 minutes before 4 till 30 minutes past 6 in the morning; and from 30 minutes past 5 till 30 minutes past 6 in the evening.

29th. From 15 minutes before 3 till 30 minutes past 5 in the morning; and from 30 minutes past 4 till 30 minutes past 5 in the evening.

October 3d. From 3 till 15 minutes before 6 in the morning; and from 15 minutes before 5 till 15 minutes before 6 in the evening.

12th. From 15 minutes past 2 till 5 in the morning; and from 15 minutes before 4 till 30 minutes past 4 in the afternoon.

18th and 19th. From 30 minutes past 1 till 4 in the morning; and from 15 minutes before 3 till 30 minutes past 4 in the afternoon.

November 10th and 11th. From 30 minutes past 12 at night till 15 minutes past 3 in the morning; and from 30 minutes past 1 till 30 minutes past 2 in the afternoon.

15th and 16th. From 12 at night till 15 minutes before 3 in the morning; and from 15 minutes past 1 till 2 in the afternoon.

29th and 30th. From 15 minutes past 11 at night till 2 in the morning; and from 1 till 15 minutes before 2 in the afternoon.

December 8th and 9th. From 15 minutes past 10 at night till

1 in the morning; and from 30 minutes past 12 at noon till 30 minutes past 1 in the afternoon.

14th 15th and 16th. From 10 at night till 15 minutes before 1 in the morning; and from 15 minutes before 12 till 30 minutes past 12 at noon.

23d and 24th. From 15 minutes past 11 till 12 at noon; and from 15 minutes past 9 till 12 at night.

28th. From 15 minutes past 10 till 11 in the morning; and from 9 till 15 minutes before 12 at night.

We do not presume to assert that every lady born on the last mentioned times, will be exempt from all descriptions of trouble during the whole of their lives, but that they will never (in spite of whatever may happen to befall them) sink below mediocrity. Even servants and those born of poor parents will possess some superior qualities—get into good company—be much noticed by their superiors, and will, in spite of any intervening difficulties, establish themselves in the world, and rise much above their sphere of birth.

It has often been recorded, and though a singular observation, experience has shown it to be a true one, that some event of importance is sure to happen to a woman in her thirty-first year, whether single or married; it may prove for her good, or it may be some great evil or temptation; therefore we advise her to be cautious and circumspect in all her actions. If she is a maiden or widow, it is probable she will marry this year. If a wife, that she will lose her children or husband: she will either receive riches or travel into a foreign land: at all events, some circumstance or other will take place during this remarkable year of her life, that will have great effect on her future fortunes and existence.

The like is applicable to men in their forty-second year, of which so many instances have been proved that there is not a doubt of its truth: Observe always to take a lease for an odd number of years; even are not prosperous. The three first days of the moon are the best for signing papers, and the first five days as well as the twenty-fourth for any fresh undertaking. But we cannot but allow that a great deal depends on our own industry and perseverance, and by strictly discharging our duty to God and man, we may often overcome the malign influence of a bad planet, or a day marked as unlucky in the book of fate.

HOW TO TELL WITH A PACK OF CARDS

WHICH OF THREE LADIES HAS THE BEST HUSBAND.

In a company in which there are three married ladies, you offer by certain mysterious calculations, to find out which of them has

the best husband.   You take any twenty-two cards from the
pack, give seven of them to each of the three ladies, and keep the
twenty-second for yourself.   Each lady now counts the spots upon
her cards, the ace counting for eleven, the king for four, the queen
for three, the knave for two, and the rest of the cards according
to their spots, the ten for ten, and the nine for nine, etc.

Let each lady now divide the number of spots upon her cards,
by the number of spots upon the card which you have retained,
and write the quotient upon the corner of a triangle drawn upon
the table.   For example, the first lady has 19 spots upon her
cards; the second, 32; the third, 54.   The card retained by you,
has 6 spots; accordingly, the quotient obtained by the first lady
(6 into 19), is $3\frac{1}{6}$, that obtained by the second (6 into 32), is $5\frac{2}{6}$,
that obtained by the third (6 into 54), is 9.   These three quotients,
written in the corner of a triangle, make a figure like Fig. 1.

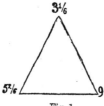

Fig. 1.

You now add together the two numbers, which stand on the
same side of the triangle, and write the sum midway between
them.

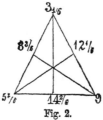

Fig. 2.

9 and $3\frac{1}{6}$ is $12\frac{1}{6}$, which is written at the side to the right; $5\frac{2}{6}$
and $3\frac{1}{6}$ is $8\frac{3}{6}$, which is written on the left side; $5\frac{2}{6}$ and 9 is $14\frac{2}{6}$,
which is written on the lower side, so that the triangle has now
the appearance of Fig. 2.

You now request each lady to add her quotient to the number
which stands directly opposite to it.   The lady who has obtained

the quotient $3\frac{1}{2}$, adds to it $14\frac{2}{3}$, and obtains the sum of $17\frac{2}{3}$; the one whose quotient was $5\frac{2}{3}$, adds to it the opposite number $12\frac{1}{4}$, and obtains also $17\frac{2}{3}$; lastly, the lady whose quotient was 9, adds to it the opposite number, $8\frac{7}{3}$, and obtains also $17\frac{2}{3}$, from which it follows that all have equally good husbands. This result is invariably the same, select what cards you please: and, after all, it could hardly be otherwise, for all men are certainly—angels.

CHARMS AND CEREMONIES.

THE CHARMS OF ST. CATHERINE.

THIS day falls on the 25th of November, and must be thus celebrated. Let any number of young women, not exceeding seven or less than three, assemble in a room, where they are sure to be safe from interlopers; just as the clock strikes eleven at night, take from your bosom a sprig of myrtle, which you must have worn there all day, and fold it up in a bit of tissue paper, then light up a small chafing dish of charcoal, and on it let each maiden throw nine hairs from her head, and a paring of her toe and finger nails, then let each sprinkle a small quantity of myrtle and frankincense in the charcoal, and while the odoriferous vapor rises, fumigate your myrtle (this plant, or tree is consecrated to Venus) with it. Go to bed while the clock is striking twelve, and you will be sure to dream of your future husband, and place the myrtle exactly under your head. Observe, it is no manner of use trying this charm, if you are not a real virgin, and the myrtle hour of performance must be passed in strict silence.

HOW TO MAKE YOUR LOVER OR SWEETHEART COME.

If a maid wishes to see her lover, let her take the following method. Prick the third, or wedding finger of your left hand with a sharp needle (beware a pin), and with the blood write your own and lover's name on a piece of clean writing paper, in as small a compass as you can, and encircle it with three round rings of the same crimson stream, fold it up, and exactly at the ninth hour of the evening, bury it with your own hand in the earth, and tell no one. Your lover will hasten to you as soon as possible, and he will not be able to rest until he sees you, and if you have quarrelled, to make it up. A young man may also try this charm, only instead of the wedding finger, let him pierce his left thumb.

APPLE PARINGS.

On the 28th of October, which is a double Saint's day, take an apple, pare it whole, and take the paring in your right hand, and standing in the middle of the room say the following verse:

St. Simon and Jude,
On you I intrude,
By this paring I hold to discover,
Without any delay,
To tell me this day,
The first letter of my own true lover.

Turn round three times, and cast the paring over your left shoulder, and it will form the first letter of your future husband's surname; but if the paring breaks into many pieces, so that no letter is discernible, you will never marry; take the pips of the same apple, put them in spring water, and drink them.

TO KNOW HOW SOON A PERSON WILL BE MARRIED.

Get a green pea-pod, in which are exactly nine peas, hang it over the door, and then take notice of the next person who comes in, who is not of the family, and if it proves a bachelor, you will certainly be married within that year.

On any Friday throughout the year—Take rosemary flowers, bay leaves, thyme, and sweet marjoram, of each a handful; dry these, and make them into a fine powder; then take a tea-spoonful of each sort, mix the powders together; then take twice the quantity of barley flour and make the whole into cake with the milk of a red cow. This cake is not to be baked, but wrapped in clean writing paper, and laid under your head any Friday night. If the person dreams of music, she will wed those she desires, and that shortly; if of fire, she will be crossed in love; if of a church, she will die single. If any thing is written or the least spot of ink is on the paper, it will not do.

TO KNOW WHAT FORTUNE YOUR FUTURE HUSBAND WILL BE.

Take a walnut, a hazel-nut, and nutmeg; grate them together, and mix them with butter and sugar, and make them up into small pills, of which exactly nine must be taken on going to bed; and according to her dreams, so will be the state of the person she will marry. If a gentleman, of riches; if a clergyman, of white linen; if a lawyer, of darkness; if a tradesman, of odd noises and tumults; if a soldier or sailor, of thunder and lightning; if a servant, of rain.

TO KNOW IF A WOMAN WITH CHILD WILL HAVE A GIRL OR BOY.

Write the proper names of the father and the mother, and of the month she conceived with child, and likewise adding all the numbers of those letters together, divide them by seven; and then if the remainder be even, it will be a girl; if uneven, it will be a boy.

TO KNOW IF A CHILD NEW-BORN SHALL LIVE OR NOT.

Write the proper names of the father and mother, and of the day the child was born, and put to each letter its number, as you did before, and unto the total sum, being collected together, put twenty-five, and then divide the whole by seven; and then, if it be even, the child shall die; but if it be uneven, the child shall live.

TO KNOW IF ANY ONE SHALL ENJOY THEIR LOVE OR NOT.

Take the number of the first letter of your name, the number of the planet, and the day of the week; put all these together, and divide them by thirty; if it be above, it will come to your mind, and if below, to the contrary; and mind that number which exceeds not thirty.

MIDSUMMER-DAY CHARM, TO KNOW YOUR HUSBAND'S TRADE.

Exactly at twelve, on Midsummer-day, place a bowl of water in the sun, pour in some boiling pewter as the clock is striking, saying thus:—

> Here I try a potent spell,
> Queen of love, and Juno tell,
> In kind union unto me,
> What my husband is to be,
> This the day, and this the hour,
> When it seems you have the power
> For to be a maiden's friend,
> So, good ladies, condescend.

A tobacco-pipe full is enough. When the pewter is cold, take it out of the water, and drain it dry in a cloth, and you will find the emblems of your future husband's trade quite plain. If more than one, you will marry twice; if confused and no emblems, you will never marry; a coach shows a gentleman for you.

A CHARM FOR DREAMING.

When you go to bed, place under your pillow a Common Prayer Book, open at the part of the Matrimonial service, in which is printed, "With this ring I thee wed," etc., place on it a key, a ring, a flower and a sprig of willow, a small heart cake, a crust of bread, and the following cards, the ten of clubs, nine of hearts, ace of spades, and the ace of diamonds; wrap all these round in a handkerchief of thin gauze or muslin, on getting into bed cross your hands and say:

Luna ever woman's friend,
To me thy goodness condescend;
Let me this night in visions see,
Emblems of my destiny

If you dream of storms, trouble will betide you; if the storm ends in a fine calm, so will your fate; if of a ring, or of the ace of diamonds, marriage; bread, an industrious life; cake, a prosperous life; flowers, joy; willow, treachery in love; spades, death; diamonds, money; clubs, a foreign land; hearts, illegitimate children; keys, that you will rise to great trust and power, and never know want; birds, that you will have many children; geese, that you will marry more than once.

THE FLOWER AUGURY.

If a young man or woman receives a present of flowers, or a nosegay from their sweetheart, unsolicited, for if asked for, it destroys the influence of the spell; let them keep them in the usual manner in cold water four-and-twenty hours, then shift the water, and let them stand another twenty-four hours, then take them, and immerse the stalks in water nearly boiling, leave them to perish for three hours, then look at them; if they are perished, or drooping, your lover is false; if revived and blooming, you will be happy in your choice.

HOW TO TELL BY A SCREW, WHETHER YOUR SWEETHEART LOVES YOU OR NOT.

Get a small screw, such as the carpenters use for hanging closet-doors, and after making a hole in a plank with a gimlet of a proper size, put the screw in, being careful to oil the end with a little sweet oil. After having done this, take a screw-driver and drive the screw home, but you must be sure and observe how many turns it takes to get the screw in so far that it will go no farther. If it requires an *odd* number of turns you can rest assured that your sweetheart does not love you yet, and perhaps is enamored of some other person; but if the number of turns is an *even* number, be happy, for your sweetheart adores you, and lives only in the sunshine of your presence.

THE MATHEMATICAL FORTUNE TELLER;

OR, HOW TO TELL ANY PERSON'S AGE.

PROCURE six cards, and having ruled them the same as the following diagrams, write in the figures neatly and legibly.

You propose to tell how old any person is, providing their age does not exceed sixty. How is this done?

Request the person to give you all the cards containing his or her age, and then add the right hand upper corner figures together, which will give the correct answer. For example: Suppose the person's age is 20, the cards with 4 and 16 in the corners will be given, which makes the answer 20, and so on with the others.

3	5	7	9	11	1
13	15	17	19	21	23
25	27	29	31	33	35
37	39	41	43	45	47
49	51	53	55	57	59

5	6	7	13	12	4
14	15	20	21	22	23
28	29	30	31	36	37
52	38	39	44	45	46
47	53	54	55	60	13

9	10	11	12	13	8
14	15	24	25	26	27
28	29	30	31	40	41
42	43	44	45	46	47
56	57	58	59	60	13

3	6	7	10	11	2
14	15	18	19	22	23
26	27	30	31	34	35
38	39	42	43	46	47
50	51	54	55	58	59

17	18	19	20	21	16
22	23	24	25	26	27
28	29	30	31	48	49
50	51	52	53	54	55
56	57	58	59	30	60

33	34	35	36	37	32
38	39	40	41	42	43
44	45	46	47	48	49
50	51	52	53	54	55
56	57	58	59	60	41

CPSIA information can be obtained
at www.ICGtesting.com
Printed in the USA
LVHW041504040419
612996LV00001B/16/P